Edited by John M. Sullivan, Jr.

THE PIPER COMPANY

Executive Offices	*West Coast Offices*
120 North Main Street	P.O. 26274, U.S. Custom House
Blue Earth, Minn. 56013	San Francisco, California 94126

Scentuous Cookery

Or How to Make It in the Kitchen

by
Jane Johnston
and
Phyllis Jedlicka

Illustrated by
G. R. Cheesebrough

Contents

Dedicated to the preservation
and encouragement of sensuous,
scentful cooking—the kind
every child enjoys without
knowing why and every adult
anticipates with flavorous
memories.

We dedicate this to our own
children whose love of good
food made us better cooks...
Scott
Paula
Wendy
Jennifer
and to Lynn.

Introduction

Deliciously over the past years my television audience has shared with me cooking secrets explained and simplified by respected professional chefs.

These skilled men and women learned their arts in many different countries — including the Island of Malta. (Malted milks, I've been told, did not originate there, but Maltese Cats and the mysterious Maltese Falcon did. Our chefs didn't suggest recipes for either.)

From the wonderfully diverse backgrounds of these professional chefs, this book has been designed to bring smiles as well as recipes including Irish coffee, cherries jubilee and tasty tricks with leftover mashed potatoes.

We've taken what we consider the best of the cooking secrets and offer them here for your enjoyment, with hints, tips, and anecdotes to make your cooking more fun and more flavorous.

Try some of them soon. I think you'll find, as we have, that you can cook up a show as well as a pro.

Jane Johnston

Jane Johnston

P.S.

One might say Eve was the first female to discover that a little food in the right place was rewarded with more than just a pat on the head. The way to a man's heart, his pocketbook and his mother may all very well be through those pots and pans in your kitchen. A few ladies we've run across have even used their culinary skills to create kingdoms for their men and themselves. Should you do less?

The helpful chefs who so graciously give you their recipes and cooking tips do not always agree on the best methods or the best recipes. A few are even a little vague in their directions. But all agree there's no greater pleasure than good eating.

We've included some favorite recipes of our own and enough food facts to make your dinner conversation simply fascinating! It's all here to help you enjoy the age old art of cookery...indeed a most scentuous art.

Phyllis Jedlicka

Phyllis Jedlicka

Chapter 1

Chefs I Have Known

The word chef *is French, meaning "chief or master," and the chefs I know are just that—chiefs of the kitchen and masters of cooking. Endowed with a special talent, they are sometimes volatile and they are always eager to talk about food. Each has an interesting background and a host of colorful stories to tell about life among the pots and pans. Here is a glimpse of just a few of the many marvelous chefs I have known.*

There was more than the luck of the Irish going for him when John Logan turned his cooking skill into a ticket around the world. At age nineteen, with five years training behind him, Chef Logan left his native Ireland and joined the P & O Lines. He spent the next five and one-half years cooking and cruising to every major seaport in the world. Today, his cooking repertoire covers four continents, yet he continues to devise new recipes. We feature six of Chef Logan's recipes here and many more throughout the book.

IRISH BARN BRACK

1 cup of tea	2 cups flour
1 cup brown sugar	1 egg
1 lb. raisins	

1. Soak sugar and raisins in tea overnight.

2. Add flour to mixture and mix well.

3. Place in breadpan and paint with 1 beaten egg. Bake 50 minutes at 350⁰.

Serves 4.

Tea time in Ireland is a delightful time of day. If you're ever fortunate enough to take tea in an Irish cottage, you may be served this favorite tea time treat. Chef Logan suggests serving barn brack either hot or cold with butter or marmalade.

OLDE FASHIONED SALMON CAKES

1 lb. can red salmon,
  drained
1 small onion
2 eggs
12 med. potatoes

chopped parsley
2 tsp. Worcestershire sauce
beaten eggs
breadcrumbs
flour

1. Finely chop parsley and onion.

2. Boil and mash potatoes. Add salmon, chopped parsley, onion and Worcestershire sauce. Add 2 eggs and mix well.

3. Shape into patties. Dip patties in flour, beaten eggs and breadcrumbs. Refrigerate for 15 minutes.

4. Deep fry until golden brown or pan fry in butter, turning occasionally, until golden brown. (When pan fried, patties must be handled with extreme care to avoid crumbling.)

Makes 6, 4 to 5 oz. patties.

STUFFED PORK CHOPS CLONMEL

6 pork chops, ¾ in. thick ½ lb. fresh mushrooms,
1 med. onion, diced   sliced
2 peeled apples, sliced   ½ lb. sausage meat
2 eggs   8 oz. fine breadcrumbs
chopped parsley   butter

Preheat oven to 350°

1. Saute diced onion and sliced mushrooms in butter.

2. When cooked, combine onion and mushroom mixture in bowl with sausage meat, apples, chopped parsley and 4 oz. breadcrumbs.

3. When cool, add 1 beaten egg. Season.

4. Slit pork chops from side ¾ way through. Put stuffing in slit. Roll stuffed chops in flour, beaten egg and remaining breadcrumbs. Brown both sides in small amount of oil in fry pan. Bake for 45 minutes.

Serves 6.

Have you ever wondered how restaurants seem to be able to keep the crumb coatings on meat but when you try it at home the crumbs fall off? Chef Logan gave us the answer—dust the meat, which has been well dried, with flour. Then dip it in beaten egg or an egg wash and then roll it in breadcrumbs. The trick is dusting it with flour first.

Chef's Tip: Egg wash

1 cup milk   salt and pepper
2 eggs, beaten

1. Mix milk and beaten eggs. Season. Makes enough for
   4 meat servings. Dust meat with flour, dip in egg wash
   and then in fine breadcrumbs. Proceed according to
   recipe. You'll need 1 cup of crumbs for this recipe.

JOHN'S BARBECUED SPARERIBS

5 lbs. spareribs (lean pork) salt and pepper
½ cup chopped onion   1½ cups ketchup
⅓ cup red wine, dry   ½ cup dark-brown sugar
3 tsp. lemon   ¼ tsp. hot pepper sauce
1 tsp. Worcestershire sauce (Tabasco)
1 tsp. mustard seed

1. Cover spareribs with the onion, wine, salt and pepper.
   Marinate for 1 hour, turning occasionally.

2. Combine remaining ingredients in saucepan. Cook,
   stirring often, for 5 minutes or until thickened.

3. String ribs accordion-style on skewer of grill and
   secure with clamps. Cook 1½ hours or until tender,
   basting the last hour with the sauce. Use a drip pan
   under the ribs. If preferred, bake on a rack in oven at
   375°.

Serves 6.

A sense of humor helps any chef through the trying times in a hectic kitchen. Chef Logan tells of one particularly difficult waiter who made a practice of upsetting the kitchen staff. Night after night the harassment went on until finally the staff decided to even the score. When the waiter came in with an order for filet of sole, Chef Logan took off his shoe, cut off the sole, covered it with batter, deep fried it and garnished it with all the trimmings. The unsuspecting waiter served the "filet of sole" and suffered the consequences. Let's hope the customer had a sense of humor too!

SPAGHETTI SAUCE WITH CLAMS

2 cloves garlic, minced
2-4 oz. jars of sliced
   mushrooms, drained
¼ cup butter or margarine,
   melted

2-7 oz. cans minced clams,
   undrained
2 Tbsp. chopped parsley
⅛ tsp. salt
⅛ tsp. cracked black pepper

1. Saute garlic and mushrooms in melted butter until mushrooms are lightly browned.

2. Stir in remaining ingredients. Cover and simmer about 10 minutes, stirring occasionally.

3. Serve over cooked spaghetti (8 oz. pkg.).

Yields 3 cups sauce. Serves 4.

Chef's Tip:
Add a few drops of oil to spaghetti as it boils. Drain spaghetti and rinse in cold water. Return to pan with melted butter and toss until coated. Now spaghetti can be kept warm without sticking.

Canned ham takes on a new elegance with Chef Logan's special glaze. It's a beautiful buffet centerpiece that you can slice and serve.

CHAUD-FROID
(Ham Glaze)

8 to 10 lb. canned ham   2 cups cream
4 cups mayonnaise   salt
2 cups water   white pepper
4 oz. plain gelatin

1. Dissolve plain gelatin in 2 cups cold water. When dissolved, heat over hot water until warm.

2. Add mayonnaise and cream and beat until smooth.

3. Strain and let cool for 15 minutes or until it thickens to a spreading consistency.

4. Dry ham and coat with glaze. Refrigerate until set. Put a second coat of the glaze on the ham, refrigerate until set.

5. When set, ham can be decorated with egg slices, sliced olives, candied fruit slices, etc.

Serves 32 to 40.

George Theros, co-owner of the Kings Inn, gives us some handy instructions for two very special foods—lobster and wild rice.

BROILED LOBSTER TAIL

Cut down back of tail. Loosen lobster meat from shell with fingers, then place back in shell. Season with a little butter and paprika and broil at 400° for about 25 minutes. Test with toothpick to determine tenderness. If lobster browns too fast, top with foil. Serve with lemon wedges and clarified butter.

Chef's Tip: Two Kinds of Lobster Tails

1. *Cold Water·*
   These dark shelled lobsters come from the Southern Hemisphere. They are preferred if available. The different varieties are Darkest Tasmanian, Dark South Australian, New Zealand and West Australian. The meat will be firm when cooked.

2. *Warm Water:*
   These lobsters have a light colored shell and are not as desirable as the cold water kind. There are spots on the shell and black skin under the meat. They will be mushy when cooked. Warm water lobsters are found in India and French Morocco.

WILD RICE

8 oz. wild rice   salt and pepper to taste
6 strips bacon, diced   pinch of sage
1 pimento, chopped fine   oil for frying
1 small onion, chopped fine

1. Wash rice thoroughly. Boil in covered pan in 3 cups of water for 30 minutes. Drain and wash rice in cold water.

2. Saute remaining ingredients.

3. Mix rice with saute mixture. Fry in hot fat, stirring constantly.

Serves 6.

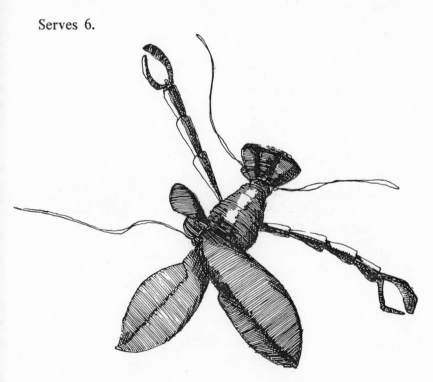

Larry Tabone from the Isle of Malta has spent most of his life in and around the kitchen as Chef, Banquet Manager and Food Director. His Spaghetti Asciuto is a nice variation for pasta. We've included more of Larry's favorites throughout the book.

SPAGHETTI ASCIUTO

4 oz. thin spaghetti
2 Tbsp. salt
3 Tbsp. oil
3 eggs, beaten
3 tsp. freshly chopped
  parsley

5 Tbsp. Parmesan or
  Romano cheese
½ tsp. freshly ground
  pepper
4 garlic cloves
oil

1. Drop spaghetti in large pot of boiling, salted water. Add 3 Tbsp. oil to prevent sticking. Boil 10 minutes. Drain and run cold water through spaghetti for 3 minutes. Drain thoroughly.

2. Mix eggs, parsley, cheese and pepper together. Fold mixture into drained spaghetti.

3. Brown 4 garlic cloves in oil in a medium-size skillet. Discard garlic. Fry half of the spaghetti at a time in hot oil. Spread the spaghetti out in the form of an omelette and turn after it has browned.

Serves 2 to 3.

A member of *Hospitality's* Hall of Fame, Clifford Warling has built quite a following at the Blue Horse restaurant. As general manager, he is responsible for everything from menu decisions to atmosphere. Cliff likes to combine romance with good food. In fact, he says that atmosphere is the single most important part of a restaurant (next to good food, of course). Keep that in mind when you try these Blue Horse recipes. A little romantic atmosphere couldn't hurt!

FETTUCINI AL'ALFREDO

1 lb. thin egg noodles	salt
2 Tbsp. melted butter	freshly ground pepper
1 cup heavy cream, hot	4 Tbsp. Parmesan cheese,
2 egg yolks, beaten	grated

1. Plunge noodles into rapidly boiling water. Cook for 8 minutes or until tender. Drain. Rinse with cold water. Drain well.

2. Toss noodles in a pan over low heat until quite dry.

3. Tossing constantly, add butter, cream and beaten egg yolks. Still tossing, add pinch of salt and pepper.

4. When mixture is quite hot add Parmesan cheese and continue tossing until well blended. Dish into individual dishes and sprinkle lightly with more Parmesan.

Serve 4 to 6.

FILET TARTARE (TARTAR STEAK)

2 lbs. ground filet of beef
(ground two or three
times)
3 egg yolks
olive oil (good grade of
French or Italian)
vinegar (French wine
vinegar)
1 Tbsp. Dijon mustard
1 Tbsp. fresh parsley,
chopped

1 Tbsp. capers
1 Tbsp. chopped onions
1 Tbsp. chopped sour
gherkins
Worcestershire sauce
4 tomatoes, quartered
anchovy filets
salt and freshly ground
pepper

1. In a flat bowl, mix with a fork egg yolks, mustard, 1 tsp. salt and fresh pepper to taste.

2. Slowly add oil and stir constantly until sauce thickens to about twice original consistency. Then mix in touch of vinegar and several dashes of Worcestershire sauce. Now mix in parsley, capers, onions and gherkins.

3. Add meat and work thoroughly with fork until well blended.

Spoon onto a platter and shape with knife into an oval or rectangular form for each serving. Garnish with sprigs of parsley and quartered tomatoes laced with anchovies.

Serve with toast or pumpernickel bread or with French fried potatoes.

Serves 4.

A chef with a kitchen in every state is Chuck Combs, who can be described most aptly as a food professional. As Director of Marketing for the Minnesota Department of Agriculture, Chuck presents food shows throughout the country using Minnesota products. His oven dinner for six is an easy way to cook everything at the same time.

CHUCK'S ROUND STEAK

2 lb. round steak, ½ in. thick
1 pkg. dry onion soup mix
2 tsp. butter (dot on top)

1. Wrap loosely in foil.

2. Bake 1 hour at 350°.

BUTTER-CUP SQUASH

3 squash   6 tsp. butter
6 tsp. honey   3 tsp. brown sugar

1. Cut squash in half. Prick with fork.

2. Add to each half: 1 tsp. honey, 1 tsp. butter, ½ tsp. brown sugar.

3. Bake 1 hour at 350°.

APPLE TREAT

6 pastry squares, 7 in.
6 med. apples, pared and cored

1. Fill apples with following mixture:
   ½ cup sugar
   1 Tbsp. butter (dot on top)
   1½ tsp. cinnamon

2. Bring points of pastry up over apples, moisten and seal.

3. Pour syrup around apples.

Bake 1 hour at 350°. Serve hot with cream.

SYRUP

1 cup sugar
2 cups water

3 Tbsp. butter
¾ tsp. cinnamon

1. Mix and boil together for 3 minutes.

Serves 6.

Bavarian born Eberhard Werthmann, like most European trained chefs, started cooking at an early age. At fourteen he became an apprentice in the kitchen working with foods "you can hurt the least." He earned $1.25 per month plus room and board during his first year, then worked his way up to Executive Chef and on to America. Today he is a Chef Instructor at a Midwest vocational high school—one of the few places in America where students can train to become chefs.

According to Chef Werthmann, foods are often named in honor of historical figures like Suzette (as in Crepes Suzette) who was the favorite entertainer of a French king. Other food names are more descriptive, like Chef Werthmann's recipe for pork chops that follows. It's just one of many recipes he shares with you in this book.

PORK CHOPS BRAISED WITH SLICED POTATOES AND TOMATOES

4-7 oz. pork chops with most of the fat trimmed
24 med. slices of potatoes, raw, ¼ in. thick
¼ No. 10 can tomatoes, crushed

1 large onion, sliced
1 clove garlic, mashed, with salt
1 good pinch of thyme

Preheat oven to 375°.

1. Saute onions in pot (use large shallow pot with cover) with very little grease.

2. Brown pork chops in frying pan, over very hot fire, and place on top of the onions, side by side.

3. Place potatoes over pork chops, add seasoning and tomatoes. Place cover on pot and bake in a hot oven until done, or approximately 15 minutes. Liquid ingredients must boil for at least 5 minutes.

4. Serve with Welsh rabbit or shirred egg dishes.

Serves 4.

In the world of professional cooking, the chef often works with a food and beverage manager who in his own right is a food expert. One of our favorites is Tom Langlais, who has made cooking a profession outside of the kitchen. Like many food pros, he seldom cooks at home but makes recipe collecting a hobby. Tom's Strawberry Orange Juice in Chapter 11 is a shining example of how easy it can be to make something different and delightful. You'll find his other contributions to this book—Chocolate Fondue in Chapter 15 and North River Road Rum Balls—equally easy and delicious.

NORTH RIVER ROAD RUM BALLS

1 cup finely crushed
  vanilla wafers (about 28)
1 cup powdered sugar
1 cup chopped walnuts
2 Tbsp. cocoa

2 Tbsp. light corn syrup
¼ cup dark rum
½ cup granulated sugar
red and green candied
  cherries

1 Combine crumbs, powdered sugar, walnuts, and cocoa; add syrup and rum and mix well.

2. Shape into 1 in. balls. Roll in granulated sugar.

3 Moisten cut side of cherry half with corn syrup and press into ball (using alternate colors).

4. Place into airtight container until ready to serve.

Makes 36 balls.

Chapter 2

Queens of the Kitchen

Very few ladies have dared to invade the male world of professional cooking. The two we feature here are not only exceptionally talented but run their own successful restaurants. While their cooking styles are as far apart as their hometowns, our queens of the kitchen have much in common. They are delightfully feminine, love to cook and are constantly trying new recipes. Here are some of their family favorites.

A phenomenal woman, with a name to match, Sra. Maria Elvira Clafira Martinez Navarro Gomez De Coronado is most affectionately known as Mama Coronado. She and her husband came to America from their native Mexico during the Roaring 20's in a Model T Ford. She spoke no English and relied on her husband to interpret for her. Today, she runs one of the Midwest's most authentic Mexican restaurants. A family enterprise, the first La Casa Coronado was opened in 1946. Mama Coronado had intended to open a pizza parlor but was persuaded to offer Mexican food instead. Since that happy decision, her restaurant has grown from four tables to service for more than ninety.

Guacamole is an avocado mixture most often found at cocktail parties, where it is served as a dip for corn chips. But guacamole can be more than a smooth, seasoned paste. Mama Coronado suggests this recipe which has a texture and flavor heavier than the more common versions made in a blender. You can add more tomatoes as she suggests and have a delightful salad. Or try our blender guacamole on p. 167.

GUACAMOLE DIP OR SALAD

¼ med. onion, peeled
1 med. tomato, peeled
   and cored
1 small hot pepper
   (optional)

3 med. avocados
½ clove garlic, crushed
2 Tbsp. lemon juice
salt to taste

1. Finely grind together onion, tomato, and if desired, a small hot pepper.

2. Blend garlic into this mixture.

3. Cut avocados in half. Remove seed and, with a spoon, scoop avocado from shell. Mash into a paste.

4. Blend all ingredients together. Add lemon juice. Mix well and salt to taste while blending.

For salads, add more chopped tomato.

AGUACATES RELLENOS DE PECHUGA
(Stuffed Avocados with Chicken)

2 med. avocados
2 heaping tsp. mayonnaise
½ tsp. olive oil
½ tsp. vinegar
1 tsp. pecans, finely
  chopped
1 tsp. onions, finely
  chopped
1 med. chicken breast,
  cooked and diced

1 hard-boiled egg, sliced
1½ roasted and
  peeled peppers, sliced
6 stuffed olives, diced
½ small dill pickle,
  diced
1 med. tomato, peeled
  and diced
lettuce

1. Combine the chicken, egg, peppers, pickle, olives, tomato, nuts and onions with the mayonnaise, olive oil and vinegar. Mix all ingredients well and salt to taste.

2. Cut avocados lengthwise and remove seeds. Peel skin from avocados with a sharp knife. On a large lettuce leaf, make a small bed of shredded lettuce on which you place an avocado half. Fill with the chicken salad and garnish with a ripe olive.

Serves 4.

Chef's Tip:
Most avocados available at your local store will be unripe. To ripen, store at room temperature for two days before refrigerating. When ripe, the avocado will yield to a soft pressure of your fingers.

CALDO DE RES
(Beef Soup)

2 lbs. beef shanks
3½ qts. water
1 No. 2½ can whole
  tomatoes
2 carrots, cut into
  1 in. pieces
2 ears of corn, cut
  into 1 in. pieces
2 large zucchini, cut
  into 1 in. pieces

1 small onion, cut
  in half
1 celery stick, cut
  into 1 in. pieces
½ med. cabbage,
  cut into 4 pieces
garlic, salt and pepper
  to taste

1. Bring water to a boil. Add meat, onion and celery.
   Add seasonings and cook until meat is tender.

2. Add vegetables and tomatoes and simmer on a low
   flame until vegetables are tender.

Serves 6 to 8.

For variety add 2 fresh green apples or 2 fresh quince that
have been peeled and cut into cubes.

CALDO DE ALBONDIGAS
(Meatball Soup)

½ lb. ground round steak
½ lb. ground veal
¾ lb. ground pork
½ cup raw rice
2 eggs
1 Tbsp. fresh coriander
  (cilantro)

¼ tsp. garlic
2 tsp. salt plus salt
  and pepper to taste
1 No. 2 can tomatoes
1 small onion, peeled
  and cut in half
1 Tbsp. oregano

1. Mix meat with rice, salt (2 tsp.) and pepper, eggs, garlic and coriander. Shape into small balls and set aside.

2. Combine in large soup pan: 3 qts. water, tomatoes, onion and oregano.

3. Heat to boiling point then drop meatballs in, one at a time. Cover and cook 30 to 40 minutes over a medium flame or until meatballs are tender and rice is cooked.

Note:
More salt may be needed for full flavor, but do this only after meat has been cooking for 15 minutes.

Serves 6 to 8.

CALAVASITAS A LA MAMA CORONADO
(Zucchini a la Mama Coronado)

2 med. zucchini squash
½ tsp. baking soda
2 eggs, separated
¼ cup flour
¾ cup cooking oil
¼ tsp. garlic powder
3 Tbsp. oil
3 med. tomatoes,
    cored and peeled

2 cups water
1 small onion, sliced
1 bell pepper, sliced
¼ tsp. black pepper
⅛ tsp. salt or
    salt to taste

1. Place squash in cold water with baking soda in saucepan. Bring to boil and remove pan from heat. Let squash set in hot water for 5 minutes.

2. Take squash from hot water and cut into 1 in. slices. Spread slices on paper towel to drain excess water.

3. Beat egg yolks until frothy. Beat egg whites with mixer until whites form peaks, then fold in egg yolks.

4. In a shallow dish, spread flour.

5. Place ¾ cup oil in skillet or electric frying pan and heat to 350°.

6. Now roll each slice of squash in flour and dip into egg batter with a fork, being careful not to tear squash. Fry in hot oil until egg is lightly brown on both sides. Remove and place on paper towel to drain excess oil.

7. Heat 3 Tbsp. oil in Dutch oven on a low flame. Add onion, pepper, garlic powder, salt and black pepper. Simmer.

8. While the above is simmering, take tomatoes plus 2 cups water and run through blender until completely blended. Add to the simmering ingredients. Cook until sauce comes to a slow boil, then add fried squash and let simmer an additional 5 minutes.

Serves 4 to 6.

FLOUR TORTILLAS

4 cups flour
⅓ cup shortening
1½ tsp. salt

1 cup warm water
4 tsp. baking powder

1. Combine all dry ingredients and cut in shortening. Add water slowly and stir until dough is soft. (Do not let dough become too wet.)

2. Knead 10 to 15 times. Divide into 12 equal pieces. Cover with cloth and let stand for 10 minutes.

3. Roll out each piece into a circle 6 in. to 8 in. in diameter. Cook on ungreased skillet until lightly brown in spots, turning once.

4. Fill with refried beans, cheese or cooked sausage. Roll up with sides tucked in and serve. (Use following recipe for refried bean filling.)

Serves 4 to 6.

FRIJOLER

1 lb. pinto beans	1 clove garlic
7 cups water	⅓ cup oil
salt to taste	

1. Soak beans in water overnight.

2. Before cooking, add garlic and enough water to cover beans and cook until tender.

3. Heat oil in heavy pan and add beans a few at a time, mashing with potato masher. (Do not use too much juice.) Simmer approximately 15 minutes over low flame, stirring constantly so beans do not stick.

4. To make refried beans, fry again in small amount of oil.

CHORIZO CON HUEVOS
(Mexican Sausage with Eggs)

3½ oz. Mexican sausage (chorizo)	2 eggs, slightly beaten salt to taste
1 tsp. oil	

1. Crumble chorizo into heated skillet with oil. Fry until sausage is well cooked.

2. Add eggs and continue to fry as if making scrambled eggs. Add a little salt to taste.

Serves 1.

Note:
If chorizo comes in a casing, remove and discard casing before frying sausage

TORTA DE HUEVO

4 eggs 2 Tbsp. oil
2 oz. corn chips, broken salt to taste
   into small pieces Cheddar cheese, grated

1. Beat eggs, add corn chips and salt.

2. Fry like an omelet in hot skillet with oil. Before egg
   sets, add a small amount of grated cheese.

Garnish omelet with sliced avocados and tomatoes.

Serves 2.

Reiko Weston left her native Tokyo in 1953 to make her home in the United States. The daughter of a naval officer, Mrs. Weston did not learn to cook until after she left home. Now she operates one of the outstanding Japanese restaurants in the Midwest, the Fuji-Ya. Overlooking the Mississippi River, the Fuji-Ya is built on the foundation of an old flour mill complete with the original six-foot thick stone walls in the basement. The restaurant's modern decor reflects the Japanese love for simple elegance. Guests sit on mats at low tables and enjoy long, leisurely meals along with the serenity of the river view.

In Japan, the family meal is often cooked at the table in a single container with each diner cooking his own portions. Meat and vegetables are cooked in sauce, in soup or on a grill. Guests are usually served a five course meal including one course of raw fish. Breakfast may be rice soup and pickles or seaweed and eggs. Students take lunch boxes to school filled with meat, rice and vegetables. Mrs. Weston tells us that small bees are a delicacy in Japan and that Japanese snacks are often rice crackers coated with a soy sauce glaze.

Before she opened the original Fuji-Ya, Mrs. Weston visited fifty Japanese restaurants around the country to taste their foods and get ideas for her own menus. She loves to experiment with foods of other nations but confines the restaurant offerings to those Japanese foods Americans seem to like most. The recipes she shares with us would make a complete four-course meal or may be enjoyed separately. Start with Sunomono Salad, then Tempura with its own dip sauce, follow with meat grilled on a hibachi and basted with Terriyaki Sauce and feature Sukiyaki. Serve plenty of hot tea and warm saki. And by all means, use chopsticks.

SUNOMONO SALAD
(Salad with vinegar dressing)

1 cup Japanese rice
  vinegar (unseasoned)
2 Tbsp. sugar (or sugar
  substitute)
2 tsp. salt
2 tsp. fresh lime or
  lemon juice

1 dash monosodium
  glutimate
mixed greens
cooked crabmeat or shrimp

1. Combine vinegar, sugar, salt, lime or lemon juice and monosodium glutimate.

2. Clean greens and break into bite size pieces.

3. Pour dressing over greens and toss. Serve salad in individual bowls and garnish with cooked or canned crab or shrimp.

Serves 4.

Chef's Note:
Japanese rice vinegar comes in two varieties—seasoned and unseasoned. Use the unseasoned variety for this recipe.

TEMPURA

1 egg
2½ cups ice cold
   water
3 cups sifted flour
raw shrimp, scallops,
   etc.

raw vegetables such as
onion, green pepper,
parsley, asparagus,
sliced squash, etc.
and mum leaves
cooking oil

1. Wash, shell and devein shrimp. Slit underside in two
   or three places to prevent curling. Cut large scallops
   into bite size servings. Clean and cut any other raw
   fish used instead of or in addition to shrimp and / or
   scallops.

2. Clean vegetables and mum leaves. Leave mum leaves
   whole. Cut onions and green peppers into rings. Slice
   squash into bite size pieces. Break parsley into bite
   size pieces. Use just the tender portion of asparagus
   and cut into bite size pieces

3. Beat egg slightly. Add ice water and mix. Add sifted
   flour. Mix lightly leaving small lumps. Batter should
   be thin.

4. Preheat oil (vegetable, corn or peanut oil) to 350°.
   Dip pieces of fish and vegetables into batter and fry to
   golden brown. Drain on paper towels.

Serve hot with tempura sauce.

Serves 4.

Chef's Note:

Tempura may be used as either an appetizer or main dish. If an appetizer, allow two pieces of fish and two to four pieces of vegetables for each serving. If used as the main dish, increase portions accordingly.

Tempura is a very light batter that takes some practice to make properly. Don't be discouraged if your first attempt is not quite what you would like. Try it several times until you develop the technique to your liking. Even your tempura "failures" are good to eat.

TEMPURA SAUCE

1 cup Dashi stock
3 Tbsp. Japanese soy
   sauce
1 Tbsp. sugar

1 Tbsp. Mirin (sweet rice wine) or Sherry
1 pinch monosodium glutimate

1. Combine above ingredients in saucepan and bring to boil.

Serve warm in individual bowls.

Serves 4.

Chef's Note:

Dashi stock is made from keip and dried katsuo (bonito). You may also use a Dashi-no-moto bag in hot water for instant Dashi.

TERRIYAKI SAUCE
(Basting sauce for fish or meat)

1 cup Japanese soy sauce
¼ cup sugar
2 Tbsp. Mirin (sweet rice wine)

1 dash red pepper (cayenne)
1 dash monosodium glutimate
1 tsp. fresh grated ginger

1. Mix ingredients together in saucepan and cook over low heat until mixture thickens. Stir occasionally.

2. Use sauce to baste meat or fish as it is broiled. Brush on sauce two or three times while broiling.

Serves 4.

Chef's Note:

Do not marinate meat or fish in basting sauce. Put raw meat or fish under broiler or on hibachi and cook for a few minutes before brushing with sauce. Continue basting as meat cooks. Marinated meat or fish has a tendency to burn quite easily. This basting method reduces the possibility of burning.

SUKIYAKI

1 cup Japanese soy sauce
1½ cup water or Dashi
½ cup sake (rice wine)

3 Tbsp. sugar
1 dash monosodium
glutimate

1 to 1½ lbs. prime rib eye, thinly sliced (meat should have some fat marbling)
1 small can yam noodles (Shirataki)
1 small can bamboo shoots

1 cup fresh mushrooms, sliced
1 medium dry onion, sliced
1 square bean curd (Tofu), cut into 8 pieces
1 bunch green onions, cut in 2 in. pieces

1. Combine soy sauce, water or Dashi, sake, sugar and monosodium glutimate for sauce.

2. Quickly saute beef slices in hot, heavy frying pan or electric frying pan. Add noodles, vegetables and bean curd. Pour in enough sauce to half cover ingredients in the pan. Simmer uncovered until the meat is about three-fourths done.

Serve with hot steamed rice.

Serves 4 to 6.

Chef's Note:
Sukiyaki may be cooked right at the table. Make half a recipe at a time so that seconds will be freshly cooked just as guests finish their first helping.

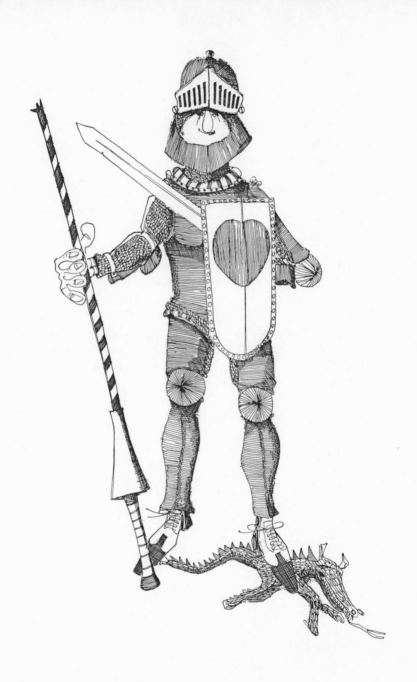

Chapter 3

Knight Time Cookery

"There is no spectacle on earth more appealing than that of a beautiful woman in the act of cooking dinner for someone she loves."
Thomas Wolfe said it and we agree. Put on your prettiest frock and whip up one of these tried and true knight pleasers. Each is made with steak and is bound to appeal to the knight in your life.

BEEF SOYA ORIENTAL

1 lb. lean top sirloin, cut in 1 in. cubes
1 Tbsp. peanut oil
small white onion, peeled, cut in thin strips
6 canned water chestnuts, thinly sliced
½ cup bamboo shoots, cut in 1 in. pieces
Large stalk celery, cut diagonally into thin strips
1 cup petit pois (fresh or frozen peas)
About 1 Tbsp. water
½ cup canned beef broth, undiluted
¼ cup soy sauce
1 tsp. sugar
½ tsp. salt (or monosodium glutamate)

1. Heat peanut oil in large skillet over high heat. Brown meat quickly on all sides in skillet. Add onions, fry lightly a few minutes. Add chestnuts, vegetables and water. Simmer uncovered 5 minutes, stirring several times.

2. Add beef stock, soy sauce, sugar and salt; simmer uncovered 10 minutes longer (or until sauce is reduced by one-half). Spoon over cooked rice or fried noodles.

Serves 4.

Serving Suggestions:
For a spicy addition add ½ tsp. star anise (available at Oriental food shops) or ½ in. piece minced, peeled, fresh ginger root to the sauce during cooking.

Tradition plays an important part in our eating habits. Oriental philosopher Lao Tze in the sixth-century B.C. discovered that improper cooking destroys the nutritional value of vegetables. He instructed his followers, the Taoists, to eat only raw or partially cooked vegetables. That tradition is still the basis of Oriental cooking. His followers are also responsible for making tea drinking a time of contemplation and enjoyment.

CARBONNADES A LA FLAMAUDE

2 lbs. boneless chuck, cut
   into 1 in. cubes
6 med. onions, sliced
2 cloves garlic, finely
   chopped
12 oz. bottle of beer
1 Tbsp. chopped parsley

1 bay leaf
¼ tsp. thyme
¼ cup salad oil
flour for dredging
salt and freshly ground
   black pepper to taste

1. Combine flour, salt and pepper. Dredge the meat in the seasoned flour.

2. Heat oil in skillet. Add onions and garlic and cook until tender but not brown. Remove onion from the skillet.

3. Add meat and brown on all sides, adding a little more oil if necessary. Combine onions with meat in skillet.

4. Add beer, parsley, bay leaf, and thyme.

5. Cover and cook over low heat until meat is tender, about 1 hour or more. Discard bay leaf. Serve with buttered noodles or boiled potatoes.

Serves 4 to 6.

BEEF STROGANOFF

2 lbs. beef tenderloin, cubed	2 oz. vodka
1 small onion, chopped	1 pt. sour cream
6 oz. can button mushrooms, sliced	2 oz. sherry wine
	salt
1 green pepper, diced	pepper
2 Tbsp. butter	monosodium glutamate
	Worcestershire sauce

1. Saute beef, onion, mushrooms, and green pepper in butter and vodka until meat is medium rare.

2. Blend sour cream with meat mixture.

3. Add sherry. Season to taste. Serve over cooked rice or noodles.

Serves 6.

Note:
Do not boil after sour cream has been added. Sour cream curdles when it is boiled.

The average American eats 114 pounds of beef every year. Yet as popular as it is today, in Shakespeare's time the English thought that consuming large quantities of beef caused stupidity and melancholy. The Japanese didn't even taste beef until 1856 and in India the Hindu religion still prohibits the slaughter of cattle for food.

INDIVIDUAL TENDERLOIN OF
BEEF WELLINGTON

4-7 oz. tenderloin of beef
4 oz. or 1 cup mushrooms
  (canned or fresh)
2 oz. or ½ cup liver pate
2 strips bacon, cut into
  4 pieces each

¼ onion, chopped
1 lb. or 4 sticks pastry
1 clove garlic
eggwash
salt and pepper

Preheat oven to 375°.

1. Char seasoned tenderloin on both sides, keeping it very rare.

2. Dice mushrooms and onion finely and add to crushed garlic to saute until cooked.

3. Add liver pate and mix thoroughly. Cool.

4. Roll out pastry into four squares approximately 8 in. each. Eggwash the pastry squares. Center each piece of tenderloin in a pastry and cover with liver pate mix. Add 2 small pieces of bacon on top. Fold in corners of each pastry to the middle, sealing well. Brush with eggwash.

5. Bake approximately 30 minutes at 375°.

Serves 4.

"Kissin' wears out, cookery don't," is a Pennsylvania Dutch saying worth remembering when you wonder if all this cooking effort is really worthwhile.

BEEF EN BROCHETTE WITH WILD RICE

16 cubes beef tenderloin   4 skewers
16 mushroom caps   season to taste
16 small cubes bacon

1. Alternate beef cubes, mushrooms and bacon on skewers (4 each to a skewer).

2. Broil in oven or outdoor grill until meat is done to liking. Serve with wild rice.

Serves 4.

WILD RICE

½ small onion, minced   4 cups chicken broth
6 mushroom caps, sliced   ¼ stalk celery, whole
4 slices bacon, chopped   1 bay leaf
2 cups wild rice, well   1 clove garlic
    washed

1. Saute onion, bacon and chopped mushrooms in pan.

2. Add remaining ingredients and bring to boil.

3. Cover and place in 450° oven for 30 minutes.

4. Remove celery, bay leaf, and garlic before serving.

Serves 4 to 6.

Brochette is the lovely French version for our own more gruesome word, *skewer*. The Turks eat kebab, and with mutton they have shish-kebab. The Near East Georgians enjoy shashlyk, the Germans spiess and the Greeks souvlakia. It all means the same thing—chunks of meat strung on a sword and broiled over a fire just as it was originated before 1000 B.C. by the Aryans of Central Asia.

SHISH-KEBAB

2 lbs. round steak	4 strips bacon, cut in
4 green peppers	1 in. pieces
16 small white onions	1 can water chestnuts
½ lb. fresh mushrooms	

1. Cube steak into 1 in. squares.

2. Remove seeds from peppers and cut in 1 in. pieces. Remove skins from onions. Clean and dry mushrooms. Drain water chestnuts.

3. Marinade steak, onions, peppers, mushrooms and water chestnuts overnight in refrigerator in a large bowl, using the Port Tufik Marinade.

PORT TUFIK MARINADE

1 Tbsp. grated fresh ginger
   root or 1 tsp. ground
   ginger
2 cloves garlic, minced
¼ tsp. cracked pepper

½ tsp. monosodium
   glutamate
½ cup soy sauce
¼ cup brown sugar
2 Tbsp. olive oil

Mix all ingredients together.

4. Prepare skewers by alternating the shish-kebab ingredients with a water chestnut on each end of skewer. Broil over hot coals 10 to 12 minutes, or to a rare or medium-rare stage, turning frequently and basting with marinade.

Serves 4.

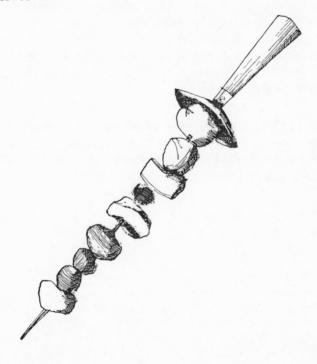

DANISH MUSTARD STEAK

4-5 oz. steaks
4 tsp. French style mustard (Dijon Mustard)
2 tsp. mild herb mustard (reg. mustard)
½ tsp. sage leaves
½ tsp. freshly grd. pepper
4 Tbsp. sour cream
2 oz. cognac or brandy

¾ tsp. paprika
¼ tsp. rosemary
1 tsp. chopped chives
½ cup whipping cream
2 oz. butter
salt to taste
flour to be sprinkled on each steak

1. Have your meatman cut four 5 oz. beef sirloin or tenderloin filets and flatten them to about ½ or ¼ in. in thickness.

2. Rub each steak with salt, pepper, rosemary, sage, half of the paprika, and sprinkle each steak with flour.

3. Saute steaks in butter in a heavy skillet for about 2½ minutes (med. rare). Remove from skillet and flambe with the cognac. Place the steaks on a serving plate and start the sauce.

4. Sauce: Mix the mustard with the remaining beef juices and cognac. Stir in the sour cream and chives and then add the whipping cream. Bring to a boil and simmer for 1 minute. Pour over steaks and serve.

Serves 4.

STEAK DIANE

2 New York cut sirloin
steaks (16 oz.)
3 Tbsp. butter
1 Tbsp. shallots, chopped
1 Tbsp. chives, chopped
3 Tbsp. A-1 Sauce

1 Tbsp. Worcestershire
sauce
1 Tbsp. prepared mustard
salt and pepper
1 Tbsp. chopped parsley

1. In a heavy skillet, melt 2 Tbsp. butter and in it gently saute shallots until golden.

2. While that is cooking, salt and pepper steaks which have been trimmed and pounded very thin. Sear steaks on both sides in skillet and remove.

3. Add to skillet remaining butter, A-1 sauce, Worcestershire sauce, chives, and mustard. Blend well over fire. DO NOT COOK SAUCE.

4. Return steaks to skillet and saute them until done to taste.

Serve on plates and sprinkle with parsley.

Serves 2.

For centuries various foods were supposed to contain aphrodisiac powers. Madame DuBarry fed Louis XV everything from sweetbreads to pheasant in wine to arouse his amorous desires. Aristotle thought peppermint oil would do the trick and Brillot-Savarin said the truffle was the magic food. Over the years the list of supposed aphrodisiacs included raw beef, carrots, cloves, Coca-Cola, eggs, garlic, mushrooms, oysters, tomatoes and dozens more. Even recently in the Union of South Africa, a Johannesburg school forbade the eating of peanuts and peanut butter as being sexually stimulating. All foods, so we're told, are miserable failures as love potions.

STEAK AND KIDNEY AND MUSHROOM PIE

4 cups cubed beef
  (1½ in. cubes)
2½ cups lamb or veal
  kidneys, cubed
3 cups finely chopped
  onions
2 bay leaves
1 Tbsp. Worcestershire
  sauce

1 clove crushed garlic
2 Tbsp. tomato paste
salt and pepper to
  taste
cold water
mushrooms, sliced
butter

1. Saute onions in Dutch oven, add beef and kidneys, then brown. Salt and pepper lightly. Add seasonings and tomato paste. Barely cover with cold water. Cover and simmer approximately 1½ hours. The mixture will reduce to required consistency.

2. When cooked, check for seasoning. Add mushrooms which have been semi-cooked in butter.

3. Put in baking dish and cover with short-paste. Bake in 375° oven for approximately 35 to 40 minutes.

Serves 6.

PASTE FOR PUDDING

2 cups flour   2 Tbsp. baking powder
1 cup chopped suet   1 egg
salt   water

1. Mix flour, salt and baking powder. Add chopped suet and fold in well. Add egg and water to required consistency. Dough must be dry but pliable.

2. Line greased pudding dish with paste, allowing enough overlapping to fold over. Cover open side with greased cloth.

If you want your favorite knight to enjoy his food, don't try to compete with the fragrance of your cooking. Heavy perfumes can be overpowering enough to distort the sense of taste. Keep your perfumes out of the kitchen and away from the table unless, of course, you would rather that he couldn't taste your cooking!

Chapter 4

How to Impress His Mother
Without Really Trying

Music, they say, will soothe the savage beast, and everyone knows that the way to man's heart is through his stomach. But no one has ever solved the problem of how to impress a mother-in-law. Until now. Here are some absolutely delicious dishes that taste like they took a lot of hard work but you'll find them a breeze to prepare. And after your mother-in-law is suitably impressed, share the recipes with her. The way to a mother-in-law's heart may be through her cookbook.

CHICKEN WITH MUSHROOM SAUCE

2½ lb. frying chicken,
  cut into serving pieces
salt and pepper
8 Tbsp. butter
1 lb. fresh button mush-
  rooms, thickly sliced

1 tsp. green onions,
  minced
1½ pts. whipping cream
2 oz. dry white wine

Preheat oven to 325°.

1. Wash and dry chicken.

2. Melt butter in heavy frying pan. Saute chicken on both sides until golden brown. Season with salt and pepper. Remove chicken to baking pan, cover and bake until tender, approximately 30 minutes.

3. Wipe mushrooms clean and slice. (Do not substitute canned mushrooms, or sauce will become greasy.) Saute mushrooms and onions over high heat in same pan used for browning chicken. (Add more butter if pan has become too dry.) Season to taste. Stir mushrooms well to coat with chicken brownings and butter. Cook until tender, approximately 10 minutes.

4. Lower the flame and add cream and wine. Adjust seasoning. Simmer until sauce thickens (15 to 20 minutes) and becomes light brown in color.

5. Pour mushroom sauce over chicken just before serving. Serve with Wild Rice A La Wendy.

Serves 4.

Note:
This sauce keeps well after it has thickened slightly. Just lower flame and keep it warm until serving time. The longer it waits, the better the flavor. Just prior to serving, heat sauce to boiling point and let it bubble for a minute or two. If it becomes too thick, thin it with more cream.

WILD RICE A LA WENDY

1 cup wild rice
2 cups chicken broth
3 cloves
1 med. onion
1 bay leaf

⅓ cup whipping cream
2 oz. dry white wine
1 Tbsp. butter
salt and pepper

1. Wash and drain wild rice three or four times to remove stones.

2. Place thoroughly washed rice in pan. Cover with chicken broth. Push cloves into peeled onion and place in center of pan. Add bay leaf. Bring to boil, cover tightly and simmer very slowly for 1 hour. Remove from heat and keep covered for an additional 15 minutes. DO NOT LIFT LID DURING THIS TIME. Remove onion, cloves and bay leaf, and discard.

3. In a separate pan, scald the cream. Add the wine and butter and stir until butter has melted.

4. Add cream mixture to wild rice and mix thoroughly. Season to taste.

Makes 3 cups cooked rice. (Wild rice triples in volume when cooked.)

Chef's Tip:
Wild rice may be kept warm for a short time over hot water in a double boiler or covered in a very low oven.

Wild rice really isn't rice, but grass seeds of an aquatic species called Zizania aquatica. The Indians introduced it to American colonists who thought it inferior to the more familiar polished rice. Today it sells from fifteen to twenty times the cost of white rice.

BREAST OF CHICKEN KIEV

3 boned chicken breasts
¼ tsp. black pepper
1 tsp. chopped onions
¾ cup flour
6 tsp. chilled butter

2 beaten eggs
½ cup milk
1½ cups breadcrumbs
fat for frying

1. Skin chicken breasts and cut in half lengthwise. Pound to flatten out. Sprinkle with salt and pepper.

2. Mix chilled butter and chopped onion together. Place tsp. of mixture in center of each breast. Fold ends over butter carefully (envelope style) and seal edges with toothpicks.

3. Refrigerate chicken breasts for 1 hour.

4. Flour breasts, dip in beaten egg mixed with milk, and roll in breadcrumbs. Fry in 4 in. of fat at 375° until golden brown (approximately 15 minutes). Serve with rice.

Serves 6.

RACK OF LAMB

8 rib rack of lamb   ¼ tsp. monosodium
  (2 to 3 lbs.)   glutamate
¼ tsp. ground thyme   ¼ tsp. salt
¼ tsp. black pepper   3 tsp. prepared mustard

Preheat oven to 375°.

1. Combine seasonings and rub on lamb. Then lightly brush on mustard.

2. Place lamb on rack in shallow pan, fat side up. Bake for 50 minutes or to desired doneness. Serve with mint jelly.

Serves 4.

Lamb with its decorative "panties" is a trifling of pretense compared with some of the masterpieces of merry old England. In the 14th century, King Richard II served guests gilded swans. The birds were first skinned, feathers and all, then roasted whole and dressed again in their original plumage which had been gilded. That's the hard way to impress your mother-in-law—or anyone!

LAMB LEWIE

2 lamb racks
½ cup English mustard
2 cups white breadcrumbs
½ cup butter

½ cup chopped parsley
2 cloves fresh garlic
salt and pepper

Preheat oven to 375°.

1. Mix breadcrumbs, parsley, crushed garlic, salt and pepper.

2. Cook lamb in oven for 20 to 30 minutes.

3. Remove from oven, brush with prepared English mustard. Sprinkle heavily with bread mix. Sprinkle with melted butter.

4. Return to oven and cook to golden brown or desired degree of doneness.

Serves 6.

Garlic, so often associated with Italian cooking, was first popular with the Egyptians and then with the Chinese. Early Greek, Roman and Indian cultures avoided it and still do today. The Greeks rely on basil as their chief seasoning, curry is the favorite in India and most Italians prefer basil, marjoram, thyme and oregano to garlic. Ancient India outlawed garlic and onions, and the Roman Senate forbade garlic-eating citizens to enter the temple of Cybele. That sounds practical. A congregation of garlic eaters might be too much for any deity.

TENDERLOIN STEAK A LA MAISON

4 tenderloin steaks
(6 oz. each)
¾ lb. fresh mushrooms, sliced
1 med. onion, diced
½ cup red wine (dry)
¼ cup butter
4 slices bacon
2 cups brown sauce
flour
salt and pepper
4 slices bread

1. Wrap bacon slices around steaks and skewer with toothpicks. Sprinkle with salt and pepper.

2. Flour steaks and saute in butter, turning over, for approximately 12 minutes.

3. When done, remove from pan and saute onion and mushrooms until golden brown. Add red wine and brown sauce. Simmer for 5 minutes.

4. Return steaks to pan, cover and simmer for 7 minutes.

5. Trim bread slices to a round shape. Fry in butter until golden brown.

6. Place steaks on crouton (bread rounds). Pour sauce over and serve.

Try a garnish of a half tomato coated with Parmesan cheese and asparagus spears or green beans.

Serves 4.

Chef's Tip:
Sauce can be made in advance. Use your favorite brown sauce recipe.

PARMESAN TOMATO

2 tomatoes
2 tsp. Parmesan cheese

1. Cut tomatoes in half. Sprinkle with cheese.

2. Bake in 350° oven for 15 minutes.

BEEF BRISQUET A LA BABY BERMAN

4 to 5 lb. beef brisquet
paprika
2 med. onions
salt and pepper
2 cups water

2 tsp. Kitchen Bouquet
  (or more to taste)
6 potatoes (optional)
12 carrots (optional)

Preheat oven to 400°.

1. Roll brisquet and securely tie (or have it done in meat market). Season liberally with paprika. Bake uncovered at 400° for one hour. Reduce oven to 300°.

2. Season meat with salt and pepper. Cover roast with thick onion slices. Season onions. Add water and Kitchen Bouquet. Cover tightly and bake in slow oven for 2½ hours.

3. Vegetables may be added to pan during last hour. One hour before roast is done, add carrots which have been scraped clean. Thirty minutes later add potatoes which have been peeled and quartered. Season each vegetable as it is added. (Vegetables may take longer depending on size.) Serve sliced meat with vegetables and pass plenty of sauce just as it comes from the pan Adjust seasoning if necessary.

Serves 6 to 8.

BALL GAME BEEF STEW

2 lbs. raw stew meat
5 sticks celery, diced
  in large pieces
5 carrots, cut in
  3-inch chunks
5 med. potatoes,
  cut in thirds

1 med. can green
  beans and juice
1 med. can small whole
  onions and juice
1 large can tomatoes
½ cup tapioca (uncooked)
3 tsp. salt

Preheat oven to 275º.

1. Mix all ingredients together in large casserole.

2. Cover and bake for 6 hours.

Serves 8.

Yes, this stew does cook for six hours. Long enough for you to go to a ball game, clean the house, have your hair done, mow the lawn or go scuba diving. Both the stew and brisquet recipes are designed to let your dinner cook while you impress everyone with your other talents. Then like magic you whisk dinner from the oven to the table. Have some cold vichyssoise (p. 182) in the refrigerator for openers and close with flaming cherries jubilee (p. 212). You might even throw in a few popovers (p. 188) to prove you are indeed a cooking genius.

TURKEY CORDON BLEU

2 slices of turkey
white meat (raw)
2 or 3 slices of boiled
ham, sliced thin
2 or 3 slices of provo-
lone or Swiss cheese

¼ cup supreme sauce
1 large mushroom cap
flour, salt and pepper

Preheat oven to 350°.

1. Dredge turkey in seasoned flour, salt and pepper. Saute in butter. Brown on both sides to a golden brown. Bake for 5 to 7 minutes.

2. Remove from oven and cover turkey with the slices of ham. Top with supreme sauce and cheese. Return to oven until cheese melts and turns a golden brown.

3. Serve with a mushroom cap as a garnish on top.

Serves 1.

Chef's Tip:
Supreme sauce is white sauce made with ⅓ cup cream and ⅔ cup chicken stock instead of milk.

OYSTERS ROCKEFELLER

12 oysters in shell
8 oz. pkg. frozen spinach
1 heaping Tbsp. flour
1 heaping Tbsp. butter,
 melted
1 cup milk, heated
¼ tsp. salt
paprika
dash black pepper

few drops Tabasco sauce
few drops Worcester-
 shire sauce
¼ fresh garlic clove,
 diced
3 Tbsp. grated Cheddar
 cheese
parsley
1 lemon, cut in wedges

Preheat oven to 425°.

1. Wash oysters in cold running water before opening. Leave on half shell.

2. Cook spinach according to package directions, making sure it is well done.

3. Saute flour and butter in hot pan. Add hot milk and blend until creamy.

4. Drain spinach and chop. Add cream sauce, salt, black pepper, Tabasco, Worcestershire and garlic.

5. Spoon over oysters. Then sprinkle with grated cheese and a few drops melted butter. Top with paprika.

Place oysters in pan in oven for 15 to 20 minutes. Garnish with lemon wedges and parsley. Serve hot with salt and pepper.

Serves 4.

This sumptuous dish originated in the famous New Orleans restaurant, Antoine's, in 1899. Supposedly, a customer tried the new dish and said "It's rich as Rockefeller." Had it been invented in more modern times it might have been called "Oysters Getty" or "Oysters Onassis" or maybe even "Oysters Hughes."

Contrary to popular belief, oysters can be eaten any month, even months that do not contain *R*. The myth arose due to the fact that English oysters taste gritty during the summer spawning months. American oysters, however, do not change in flavor and are enjoyed throughout the year on the Pacific coast.

LOBSTER THERMIDOR

4-8 oz. lobster tails
1 Tbsp. salt
6 large fresh mushrooms,
    diced
1 med. size green pepper,
    diced
1 pimento, diced
4 Tbsp. melted butter

4 Tbsp. flour
1 cup hot milk
1 cup hot cream
1 tsp. salt
¼ tsp. white pepper
4 egg yolks
¼ cup sherry wine
Parmesan cheese

Preheat oven to 375°.

1. Boil lobster tails in water with 1 Tbsp. salt for 20 minutes.

2. Remove from boiling water and chill in cold water.

3. Split lobster tails, remove meat and dice to bite size. Reserve tails for stuffing.

4. Saute green peppers and mushrooms in 4 Tbsp. butter, but do not brown. Add 4 Tbsp. flour and stir until well mixed. Add hot milk and cream and stir continuously until smooth and thick. Add lobster meat and diced pimento and heat thoroughly. Season.

5. Remove from fire, then add egg yolks and sherry wine which have been beaten together and stir into lobster mixture.

6. Stuff shells and sprinkle generously with Parmesan cheese, bits of butter and sprinkle with paprika.

7. Bake in 375 to 400° oven until golden brown.

Serves 4.

LOBSTER & CAPON KNICHERBOCKER

1 cup diced cooked
  lobster meat
1 cup diced cooked
  capon meat
3 oz. butter
½ cup sherry wine

½ tsp. paprika
4 egg yolks beaten
  lightly
1⅓ cup cream
1 Tbsp. cognac

1. Combine lobster, capon, paprika and butter. Saute for 3 or 4 minutes, add sherry and cook until wine has almost completely disappeared.

2. Combine cream and egg yolks and add to mixture. Stir constantly until sauce is smooth and thick. Do not boil.

3. Add cognac.

Serve over saffron rice.

SAFFRON RICE

1 cup converted rice
1½ cups boiling water

1 tsp. salt
3 sprigs saffron

1. Combine all ingredients and cook (covered) over boiling water about 40 minutes. Rice should be tender and grains separate.

Serves 4.

MOCK DUCK ON GREEN NOODLES

3 lbs. pork tenderloin   4 oz. pork sausage
1 onion, chopped   salt
sage   pepper
garlic   2 eggs, slightly beaten
2 cups breadcrumbs

Preheat oven to 375°.

1. Saute onions, garlic and sage until onions are soft, not brown.

2. Add to breadcrumbs and sausage. Mix thoroughly. Add salt, pepper, and eggs. Mix. If mixture is dry, add milk to moisten.

3. Slit tenderloin. Fill with dressing. Bind with string. Season with salt and pepper. Roast in oven for 30 minutes at 375° or until done.

4. Slice and cover with Marsala sauce. Serve over green noodles.

Serves 6.

Note:
Marsala sauce may be made with a basic brown sauce to which you add Marsala wine. Boil down ¼ cup of wine and add 1 cup brown sauce. Simmer and adjust seasonings.

Add a tablespoon or two additional wine if necessary.

Just before serving, stir in 1 Tbsp. butter.

Women throughout history have used food to gain all sorts of things—men, kingdoms, wealth, jobs, power, etc. Agrippina, it is said, fed poisonous mushrooms to Emperor Claudius and gained an empire for her son Nero. Henry VIII's last wife, Catherine Parr, simply made sure the king's gluttonous appetite was well supplied and let him eat himself into oblivion and out of her way. Marie Antoinette, had she been able to curb King Louis XVI's eating binges, might have saved her neck from the guillotine. Instead, she and the king were captured when he interrupted their escape to enjoy a three-hour lunch. In the 17th centrury, Nell Gwynn sold oranges in theaters and went on to become a famous actress and mistress of Charles II. This might be as good a place as any to mention that Eve had a way with food, too. You'll also be happy to learn that she didn't feed Adam an apple but more likely an apricot or banana. Historians seem undecided as to which it was, but they do agree it wasn't an apple. It's just as well we didn't learn this shattering news sooner. Somehow Adam's apricot or Adam's banana doesn't seem as suitable as Adam's apple.

Chapter 5

Variations on a Chicken

What is more traditional than fried chicken on Sunday? Not to mention baked chicken, stewed chicken, barbecued chicken and fricassee of chicken. In fact, chicken has probably been on your menu so often you could cluck! Don't despair. Read on for some very unfowl-like chicken.

CHICKEN KIEV

2 chicken breasts, boned	eggwash
4 oz. Maitre d' butter	flour and breadcrumbs

1. Have meatman bone large chicken breasts and split in half.

2. Place one portion of Maitre d' butter in each breast and cover with chicken.

3. Place filled breasts in freezer and allow to set for 30 minutes.

4. Roll cold chicken breasts in flour. Then dip in eggwash and roll in breadcrumbs.

French fry until golden brown, or saute in butter and bake in 375° oven for 20 to 25 minutes.

Serves 2.

Maitre d' butter:

Soften 4 oz. butter. Season with salt, pepper, dash of lemon juice and chopped parsley. Shape to fit inside chicken breasts. Freeze.

The origin of Chicken Kiev is the third largest city of the Soviet Union and largest city of the Ukraine, Kiev. The traditional recipe calls for unseasoned butter. Both recipes in this book (the one above and the one on p. 69) make a more flavorful Chicken Kiev.

Serve it with fresh garden peas, thin crisp French fried potatoes and you'll have a favorite Ukranian meal. Start with borsch and end with varenyky for a more complete Ukranian fare. Borsch is a beet soup and varenyky are dessert dumplings filled with cheese or fruit.

CRUNCH TOPPED ORIENTAL CHICKEN

1¼ lb. can pineapple chucks in heavy syrup
¼ cup (½ stick) butter
¼ cup chopped green pepper
¼ cup sliced celery
¼ cup chopped onion
¼ cup firmly packed light brown sugar
2½ Tbsp. cornstarch
½ tsp. salt
2 Tbsp. soy sauce
¼ tsp. Worcestershire sauce
2 cups liquid
1 broiler-fryer chicken (about 2½ to 3 lbs. cut up)
shaved coconut

Preheat oven to 375°.

1. Drain pineapple, reserving syrup. Add water to syrup to make 2 cups liquid. Set aside.

2. In a 2 qt. saucepan melt butter. Add green pepper, celery and onion. Saute 2 to 3 minutes. Stir in brown sugar, cornstarch and salt. Remove from heat, and stir in soy sauce, Worcestershire sauce and reserved liquid.

3. Cook over medium heat, stirring constantly until thickened. Remove from heat and add pineapple.

4. Place chicken, skin-side up, in a 13x9x2 in. baking pan. Pour sauce over all. Bake for 1¼ hour or until tender.

5. Remove chicken to a heated plate. Serve pineapple sauce over hot rice and top with shaved coconut.

Serves 4 to 6.

CHICKEN A LA PHYLLIS MARIE

2½ lb. frying chicken, cut into serving pieces
butter
salt and pepper
paprika

12 oz. jar apricot preserves
2 tsp. soy sauce
⅓ cup sliced almonds, toasted

1. Wash and dry chicken. Brown chicken in butter and season to taste with salt, pepper and paprika. Cover and simmer for 30 minutes or until tender.

2. Combine apricot preserves and soy sauce. Pour over chicken and simmer over low heat 5 minutes. Watch carefully as mixture will caramelize quickly.

3. Sprinkle with toasted almonds and serve.

Serves 4.

"A chicken in every pot and two cars in every garage" was a political slogan attributed to Herbert Hoover. The phrase Hoover actually coined didn't mention chicken but history seems determined to ignore that fact. The saying can also be traced back to the reign of Henri II of France. His wife, Catherine de Medici of Florence, brought Italian chefs to the French court as part of her dowry and established the basis for French cooking as we know it today. Henri's son-in-law, Henri IV, wished that every peasant in his realm could "have a chicken in his pot every Sunday."

BREAST OF CHICKEN PARISIENNE
with Rice Pilaf

4 chicken breasts   paprika
4 Tbsp. butter   1½ oz. sherry wine
4 Tbsp. flour   1 qt. chicken stock
salt   1 unpeeled orange cut
pepper   in sections

Preheat oven to 450°.

1. Brush chicken breasts with melted butter. Season with salt, pepper, paprika.

2. Bake at 450° for 15 to 20 minutes.

3. Remove chicken from pan and place in baking dish.

4. In same pan, heat butter, then add flour and blend well to a paste. Add chicken stock and wine. Cook 5 minutes then pour over chicken in baking dish.

5. Place orange sections around chicken and bake 1¼ hours at 375°.

Serve with Rice Pilaf.

Serves 4.

RICE PILAF

1 cup rice
4 Tbsp. chopped onion
3 Tbsp. melted butter

1 cup chicken stock
(bouillon cubes can
be substituted)

1. Add rice and onion to melted butter in pan or baking dish. Cook 1 minute, then add chicken stock.

2. Cover and bake in 375° oven for 45 minutes.

CHICKEN VESUVIO

2 frying chickens
3 eggs, beaten
1 Tbsp. parsley
1 tsp. oregano
½ cup milk
1 cup grated Parmesan
cheese

2 green peppers, cut
in strips
4 med. potatoes, sliced
salt and pepper
1 cup flour

Preheat oven to 350°.

1. Cut fryers into 8 pieces each, omitting the wings. Salt and pepper generously. Roll in flour lightly. Dip chicken pieces into a batter consisting of the 3 eggs, parsley, oregano and milk.

2. Spread 1 cup of grated Parmesan cheese in a deep soup dish and roll chicken portions in it. Fry in very hot grease until brown.

3. Put chicken into a casserole and cover with strips of green pepper and potato slices. Add ½ cup water to bottom of pan. Bake at 350° for 1 hour.

Serves 6 to 8.

CHICKEN ITALIENNE

3 lb. frying chicken
¼ cup butter or margarine
1 tsp. Italian seasoning
½ tsp. salt
⅛ tsp. garlic powder
¼ lb. mushrooms
¼ lb. bacon, diced

¼ tsp. black pepper
1 cup milk
1 cup canned tomatoes
  or tomato juice
1 Tbsp. flour
2 Tbsp. water

1. Cut chicken into serving pieces. Brown on all sides in butter.

2. Combine seasonings, milk, tomatoes, mushrooms and bacon, and pour over chicken.

3. Cover and simmer 45 minutes, or until chicken is tender.

4. Remove chicken to serving dish. Blend flour and water together. Add to liquid in skillet. Simmer over low heat, stirring until sauce thickens. Pour over chicken.

Serves 4.

CHICKEN MARENGO

1 frying chicken, med. size (sectioned)

1 med. onion, finely chopped

½ lb. fresh mushrooms, sliced

6 peeled tomatoes, chopped, or 3 cups chopped canned tomatoes

touch of garlic

½ cup white wine, dry

Preheat oven to 350°.

1. Flour chicken, saute in butter 5 minutes (turning). Then place in casserole.

2. Saute onion, mushrooms, touch of garlic. When cooked, add tomatoes, salt, and pepper to taste. Add white wine and reduce to low heat for 10 minutes.

3. Pour sauce over chicken in casserole and bake for 25 minutes.

This can be served with turned fried egg and croutons.

Serves 4.

Chicken Marengo was named in honor of a battle fought June 14, 1800, in which Napoleon Bonaparte was victorious over the Austrians. In fact, the dish was cooked right on the battlefield by his master chef, Dunand, out of the only provisions his staff could muster—three eggs, four tomatoes, six crayfish, a small hen, garlic, oil, a saucepan and some borrowed brandy.

The dish was an instant hit with the great general. But Dunand was not pleased with the crayfish-chicken combination and sometime later tried to improve the dish by substituting wine and mushrooms for the fish and brandy. Napoleon would have none of it and insisted the crayfish be included. To this day it is traditional to garnish Chicken Marengo with crayfish. We, however, prefer the improved version that is given on the previous page.

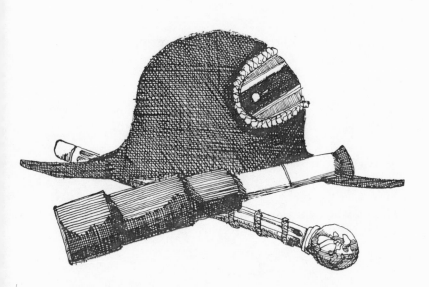

CHICKEN CACCIATORA

2½ lb. frying chicken,
  cut into serving pieces
¼ cup olive oil
¼ cup butter
1 large onion, diced
1 No. 2½ can tomatoes

6 oz. tomato juice (optional)
1 lb. button mushrooms,
  thickly sliced
salt and pepper
½ tsp. oregano
½ cup dry white wine

1. Wash and dry chicken. Brown chicken in olive oil and butter in heavy frying pan, and season with salt and pepper. Remove from pan.

2. Saute onion in the same frying pan used for browning chicken. Add tomatoes and mash into small pieces. Simmer for 5 to 6 minutes, then add tomato juice.

3. Wipe mushrooms clean with damp cloth and quarter or thickly slice. Add to sauce. Season with salt, pepper and oregano.

4. Add browned chicken to sauce, cover pan and simmer until chicken is tender, 25 to 30 minutes. Turn chicken at least once.

5. Add wine and simmer 5 additional minutes. Serve chicken with sauce and cooked spaghetti.

Serves 3 to 4.

Note:
This may be kept warm for a while before serving. In fact, it will even improve the flavor.

DEVILED SPRING CHICKEN

3 chickens (about 2 lbs.
  each), halved
½ lb. fresh breadcrumbs
  (white)
1 handful chopped parsley

3 tsp. dry mustard
3 cloves of garlic, minced
3 oz. melted butter
salt and pepper to taste
white wine

Preheat oven to 380°.

1. Cut chicken in half, cut the backbone out and press chicken together. Season with salt and pepper. Roast in 380° oven with skin side down for 30 minutes. Then turn chicken skin side up.

2. Make paste out of dry mustard and white wine. Brush the skin side of the chicken with this paste. Put the breadcrumbs mixed with garlic and parsley on the top of chicken (cover it well). Sprinkle melted butter on top of it.

3. Bake chicken at 420° until golden brown. This may be served with grilled tomatoes and bacon.

Serves 6.

CHICKEN L'DIFFERENCE

2½ lb. chicken

1. Bend chicken legs to side of bird. Follow Figure 1 dotted line, cutting between breast and legs.

2. Hold breast flat on table and pull legs backwards 180 degrees thus flattening the chicken as in Figure 2.

3. Season and roast chicken 30 minutes in 400° oven until golden brown and done.

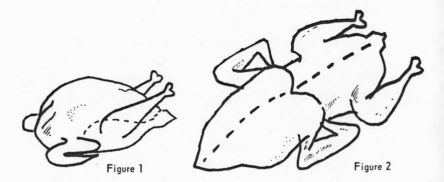

Figure 1   Figure 2

Note:
We've included this idea to give you a variation in how to change the looks of your chicken when it is served. Season and baste it to your liking. Serve it surrounded with vegetables or on a bed of rice.

When you're tired of chicken in any shape or form try roasting a Long Island duckling. Use any standard duckling recipe and baste the bird with this orange glaze. It's very un-chicken.

ORANGE GLAZE
FOR ROAST LONG ISLAND DUCKLING

1 cup fresh orange juice   1 oz. Grenadine syrup
1 Tbsp. sugar   3 Tbsp. cornstarch
1 oz. Cointreau liquor   3 Tbsp. water

1. Add sugar to orange juice in saucepan and bring to a boil.

2. Dissolve 3 Tbsp. cornstarch in 3 Tbsp. water and then add slowly to orange juice, stirring constantly until it thickens. Boil 1 minute.

3. Remove from fire and add the Cointreau liquor and Grenadine syrup.

4. Baste duckling with glaze while roasting.

Chapter 6

Norwegian Reindeer and other foreign favorites

Is there anything more exasperating than cooking for the self-styled gourmet? Next time you are faced with this dilemma, try one of these. We're willing to bet even the most travelled eater will be suitably impressed with Norwegian Reindeer, Suri Leberli or Graved Laks. The more well-known foreign favorites are good eating, too.

ROAST NORWEGIAN REINDEER

10 lb. leg of reindeer
  (or venison)
1 lb. salt pork (for
  larding)
1 large onion
4 med. carrots
2 stalks celery
1 small bunch parsley
3 to 6 bay leaves

salt and pepper
¼ lb. Norwegian goat
  cheese (optional)
½ cup Lingonberries
  (optional)
½ pt. whipping cream
¼ lb. butter
2 cups flour

Preheat oven to 350º.

1. Remove shank bone of leg and saw or chop into 2 in. pieces. Add knuckle of veal, preferably cut in the same manner. Brown in skillet, add vegetables, 3 qts. of water and bring to a moderate boil. (Cook for 2 to 3 hours, reducing liquid to half.) Prepare this meat stock ahead of time for use with roast.

2. Lard roast with ½ finger-size pork. Rub with salt and pepper. Sear in iron skillet, sealing in juices. Put into roasting pan. Add meat stock. Bake at 350°, 20 to 24 minutes per pound. Baste occasionally. For extra flavor, add ¼ lb. Norwegian goat cheese and ½ cup Lingonberries. Use roux to make sauce (¼ lb. butter and 2 cups flour), add pan drippings and strain, but first let roux cook well. To sauce add ½ pt. whipping cream, strain through cheese cloth and serve with meat. Wild rice goes well with this and turns it into a gourmet treat.

Serves 10 to 15.

While the enjoyment of reindeer meat may have a limited following, consumption of venison is as old as King Solomon, who enjoyed fallow deer and wild goat back in 9 B.C. He supposedly had seven hundred wives and three hundred concubines, so eating deer and goat can't be too disastrous.

Always avid meat-eaters, the English enjoyed venison for centuries, raising it in the kings' forests and baking it in pastries.

NORWEGIAN ROAST FRESH HAM

1 fresh ham with skin on
   (12 to 14 lbs.)
6 bay leaves, small
1 doz. whole cloves
1 Tbsp. pepper

2 Tbsp. salt
2 stalks celery
3 small onions
4 carrots
6 sprigs of parsley

Preheat oven to 250°.

1. Score ham through skin. Mix salt and pepper together and rub half into pork all around. Put whole cloves and bay leaves between cuts. Bake ham in 250° oven for 30 minutes. Then increase temperature to 350°. When skin has cooked to a crisp texture, remove and save for garnish. Sprinkle remaining salt and pepper over roast, drain all fat, and continue cooking in 400° oven.

2. Add a pint of meat stock or water and begin basting as roast begins to brown. As it becomes a golden brown, turn the temperature back to 350°, adding liquid to give the desired amount for sauce. Baste the roast intermittently. Ham must be well cooked (at least 5 hours).

Serve with sweet-sour cabbage and ham sauce. (See following page.)

Serves 15 to 20.

HAM SAUCE

Forty-five minutes before serving time, make sauce by draining liquid from roast. Have roux ready (¼ lb. butter and 2 cups flour with enough meat juices to make about 1½ qts). Save the balance of the roux in case you do not like the thickness of the sauce. Cook sauce 30 minutes, then skim off fat. Add 2 Tbsp. Coleman's mustard which has been stirred with cool water to resemble a smooth paste. Bring sauce to boil and serve over ham.

SWEET-SOUR RED CABBAGE

Use your favorite recipe for this. Add to each quart of liquid 1 level Tbsp. of whole caraway seed. Add crisp ham skin and ¼ cup pork fat, then cook 20 minutes.

SAUERBRATEN

4 to 6 lb. pot roast
(boneless chuck, round
or rump roast)
1 qt. wine vinegar
2 qts. water
1 Tbsp. salt
1 tsp. cracked whole
black pepper

1 Tbsp. sugar
1 onion, coarsely chopped
2 carrots, coarsely chopped
2 sticks celery, coarsely
chopped
1 Tbsp. mixed pickling
spice
½ cup red wine (dry)

1. Combine vinegar, water, spices and vegetables. Bring
to boil. Add ½ cup red wine.

2. Place meat in a large bowl, and pour hot marinade
over it. When cool, refrigerate 36 to 48 hours or more.

3. To cook, remove and dry meat, roll in flour and brown
on all sides in heavy kettle. Add 3 cups of the
marinade. Cover tightly and simmer until the meat is
done (about 2 to 3 hours depending on the meat).

4. Thicken the gravy with flour and pour over sliced
meat.

Serve hot with potato pancakes. (See following page.)

Serves 8 to 10.

For Variation:
Sour cream or red wine may be added to the sauce.

POTATO PANCAKES

3 cups grated raw potatoes, drained

2 slightly beaten raw eggs

1 small onion, chopped fine

2 Tbsp. flour

1. Mix all ingredients into batter.

2. Heat some shortening in a frying pan (about ½ inch deep).

3. With a kitchen spoon, drop batter in hot shortening, a spoonful at a time.

4. When golden brown, turn and brown other side.

Drain and serve hot.

Serves 8 to 10.

IRISH STEW

3 lbs. lamb shank, cubed
2 large onions
1 head cabbage
1 bunch of celery
2 leeks
12 small new potatoes

6 green onions
¼ cup milk
½ tsp. pepper
1 tsp. salt
chopped parsley

1. Cover meat with water and bring to a boil. At boiling point, remove from stove, drain and rinse meat with cold water.

2. Slice onions, leeks and celery, shred cabbage and place in a pot with the lamb and cover with cold water, adding salt and pepper. Bring to a boil and simmer for 1¼ hour.

3. Add the peeled potatoes and continue simmering until potatoes are cooked.

4. Add ¼ cup milk to the stew and stir. Serve in bowls with chopped parsley on top.

Chef's Tip:
The ¼ cup of milk adds "the old country touch" because it gives a nice white color to the stew.

Serves 6.

IRISH LAMB STEW

3 lbs. lamb shoulder	4 leeks
4 med. onions	4 stalks celery
4 med. potatoes	1 clove of garlic

1. Cut meat into cubes, trim off fat. Cover meat with water and parboil for 5 to 10 minutes. Discard water, rinse meat in cold water. Rinse out pan, return meat, cover with water, allowing for skimming.

2. Chop up vegetables, add to meat and bring to boil. Season with salt and pepper. Cook gently until meat is tender.

3. Remove meat to another pan. Put vegetables through a food mill or rub through a sieve. Add this to meat. Bring stew to a simmer. Ten minutes before serving, add the following (which have each been cooked separately) and strain:*

   2 doz. carrots Parisienne (shaped into small balls)
   2 doz. potatoes Parisienne (shaped into small balls)
   1 doz. tiny white onions, size of carrots and potatoes
   3 leeks. Cut white of leek diagonally into ¼ in. pieces. (Save green part for use in vegetable soup, etc. or making of stocks.) Cook leeks carefully to preserve the delicate flavor.

4. Carefully lift all ingredients into serving skillet, preserving color composition to give eye appeal. Just before serving, sprinkle stew lightly with chopped parsley.

*Save juices from vegetables for use in soups or stocks.

Serves 6 to 8.

LANCASHIRE HOT POT

6 large lamb chops
1 large onion, thinly
 sliced
1 No. 2 can peeled
 tomatoes

5 thinly sliced, cooked
 potatoes
1 tsp. salt
freshly ground pepper
1 tsp. rosemary

Preheat oven to 350°.

1. Brown lamb chops in frying pan and then line bottom of oven pan with the chops.

2. Layer the thinly sliced onions, peeled tomatoes and top with the sliced potatoes. Use seasonings between layers.

3. Bake for 35 minutes.

Serves 6.

VEAL MAURICE

4 thin slices of veal
2 thin slices of smoked
  salmon
flour
1 cup cream

2 oz. butter
white wine
chopped mushrooms
parsley

1. Lay 2 slices of veal on table. Lay smoked salmon on top. Cover with other slices of veal.

2. Flour and cook in butter over moderate heat. Turn until brown.

3. When cooked, remove from pan, add dash of white wine, chopped mushrooms and cream. Simmer for 5 minutes.

4. Add veal and simmer for 3 minutes in sauce.

Serve with chopped parsley and fried potatoes.

Serves 2.

Before refrigeration, little could be done to keep beef or any meat from spoiling. The French used wine and seasonings to cover the flavor of rotting meat. The Germans tried vinegar with some success, while the English camouflaged with garlic. Pork was the only meat that tasted good after salt curing, but some meats and fish could be smoked. But on the whole Englishmen especially enjoyed their beef right after it was slaughtered. Since the animals could not be fed easily during winter, most cattle were slaughtered in the fall. By mid-winter, there was rarely any meat left that was palatable. It was unthinkable to kill a calf for veal (as the French did), so veal wasn't sanctioned in England until the 17th century.

KALVFILET OSKAR

8 thin slices veal
6 oz. fresh mushrooms,
  sliced
touch of garlic powder
5 oz. butter

¼ cup whipping cream
1 pt. of milk, heated
¾ cup flour
1 tin crabmeat (8 oz.),
  chopped

1. Flour and saute veal slices in butter, turning until golden brown (about 5 minutes). When golden brown, remove. Return to pan after step 4.

2. Chop crabmeat, slice mushrooms, and saute in same pan until mushrooms are cooked.

3. Melt 5 oz. butter in small pot. Stir flour into butter, add hot milk, and stir until thick.

4. Add crabmeat, mushrooms, garlic powder, cream.

5. Pour over veal. Simmer for 6 to 8 minutes.

Serves 4.

ESCALOPE OF VEAL A LA OSCAR

4 escalopes of veal
(6 oz. each)
8 shrimp, cooked and
peeled
12 asparagus spears (canned
or cooked)

1 Tbsp. chopped green
onions
1 clove garlic
1 cup white wine
1 cup fresh cream
chopped parsley

1. Season and flour veal. Saute in butter. Remove from pan and keep warm.

2. Saute onion and add a little garlic.

3. Add white wine and reduce.

4. Next add cream and reduce to thick consistency.

5. Garnish veal with 2 shrimp and 3 pieces of asparagus spears. Pour sauce over all. Sprinkle with chopped parsley.

Serves 4.

ESCALLOPE OF VEAL YORKSHIRE

4 thin slices veal	½ cup flour
4 thin slices ham	3 eggs, beaten
4 fried eggs	1 lemon
8 anchovy filets	butter

1. Flour veal cutlets, dip in beaten egg and saute in butter, turning until golden brown. When cooked (approximately 5 minutes), remove veal from pan, and place on dish.

2. Saute ham slices. When brown, place on top of veal.

3. Fry 4 eggs and place on top of veal and ham.

4. Garnish with anchovies.

5. Squeeze juice from 1 lemon in pan with butter, and pour over all.

Serves 4.

VEAL A LA HOLSTEIN

4-6 oz. veal cutlets
4 eggs
2 Tbsp. flour
½ tsp. salt

16 anchovy filets
1 Tbsp. capers
2 Tbsp. butter
¼ tsp. white pepper

1. Pepper and salt cutlets on both sides. Flour lightly and place in hot skillet with butter. Saute on medium heat until golden brown, turning often.

2. While cutlets are sauteeing, fry eggs in separate frying pan.

3. When cutlets are done (4 to 5 minutes), place on plate. Put fried egg on top of each cutlet. Arrange anchovy filets crosswise. Sprinkle capers on top of eggs.

Serves 4.

Chef's Tip:
Serve veal with bouquets of vegetables. Arrange meat on a serving platter and surround with a selection of cooked vegetables, keeping each vegetable separate.

Like many recipes, this one was named for a geographic location. Holstein was a duchy in northern Germany and is now part of the West German state, Schleswig-Holstein, which is the northern section of the country. It is famous for dairy products and is the origin of black and white Holstein cattle.

VEAL SCALOPPINI TOSCA

12 slices thin veal
  about 4 in. square
  or round, free of any
  tendons
salt and pepper to taste

3 cloves garlic
olive oil
butter
½ lemon

Flour veal lightly.
Dip in the following batter:

3 freshly beaten eggs
3 tsp. of fresh chopped
  parsley

4 Tbsp. of grated Parmesan
  or Romano grated cheese
Add milk to thin

1. Brown 3 cloves of garlic in skillet, using equal parts of olive oil and butter.

2. Remove garlic cloves and fry the veal.

3. After veal is turned, squeeze ½ lemon over veal.

4. Garnish with filets of anchovies.

Serves 5 to 6.

ESCALOPE OF VEAL CORDON BLEU

3 lbs. of veal, sliced
   very thin
6 slices of ham (thinly
   sliced boiled ham)
6 slices of Swiss cheese

eggwash
breadcrumbs
flour
butter

Preheat oven to 350°.

1. Have your butcher slice veal into 12 very thin pieces, then flatten. (Veal thickens as it cooks.)

2. On each of the 6 pieces of veal, place 1 slice of ham, 1 slice of cheese, and 1 additional piece of veal. Roll and secure with string or toothpicks.

3. Roll veal rolls in flour. Dip in eggwash and roll in breadcrumbs. Brown in butter.

4. Bake 30 minutes at 350°. Garnish with fresh vegetables and serve.

Serves 6.

One of the greatest gourmets of all time, King Louis XIV of France, had a court favorite, Madame de Maintenon, who opened a girls' school that soon became famous for its classes in cookery. Graduates of the school wore blue ribbons on their dresses, and cordon bleu (blue thread or cord) became the symbol of outstanding cooks. When a school of cuisine opened in Paris in 1895, it adopted Cordon Bleu as its name. It still stands today as the ultimate in cooking instruction.

SURI LEBERLI
(Swiss Liver)

1½ lbs. calf's liver
½ cup flour
4 Tbsp. butter
1 tsp. wine vinegar
1 tsp. white wine

4 Tbsp. sour cream
salt
pepper
paprika

1. Cut calf's liver into strips, removing the skin and membrane. Roll one at a time in flour seasoned with salt, pepper, and a generous amount of paprika. Separate and dry.

2. Saute the strips in butter until they are browned, shaking and rocking the pan constantly to prevent sticking.

3. Add wine vinegar and dry white wine. Blend in the sour cream (must be room temperature). Serve sauce and liver together in a nest of rice and peas.

Serves 6.

Ever had to eat "humble pie"? In medieval England, "umble pies" were only for the socially inferior. Umbles were the heart, liver and entrails that English noblemen refused to eat and left for the poor peasants, who baked them into huge pies.

BAKED HALIBUT STEAK,
BELLA VISTA

4-8 oz. halibut steaks   1 green pepper (4 slices)
¼ cup white wine   1 med. onion (4 slices)
2 oz. butter   2 tomatoes (4 slices)
2 shallots, finely chopped   salt to taste

Preheat oven to 375°.

1. Saute chopped shallots in butter. Combine with wine in bottom of baking pan.

2. Add halibut steaks.

3. Top each steak with one slice each of onion, green pepper and tomato overlapping on top of each portion.

4. Cover with greased brown paper. Bake in 375° oven 10 to 15 minutes. After first 8 minutes, remove cover and baste fish.

Serves 4.

FILET OF WALLEYE PIKE CAPRICE

6 large filets of pike
flour
salt
pepper
butter
6 bananas
1 cup flour
2 eggs, beaten with equal
   portion water

1 cup breadcrumbs
½ cup melted butter
1 lemon, peeled and
   chopped
chopped parsley
½ cup French capers

1. Season and flour pike. Saute in butter, cooking slowly and turning once.

2. Flour peeled bananas. Dip in egg mixture and roll in breadcrumbs. Saute in butter until golden brown.

3. Mix melted butter, chopped lemon, parsley, and capers together.

4. Alternate pike and bananas on warm serving platter. Cover with sauce and serve.

Serves 6.

SALMON A LA MARINO

2 lbs. salmon (4 slices)   ½ cup parsley, chopped
1 cup breadcrumbs   1 tsp. salt
2 Tbsp. butter (soft)   ½ cup mayonnaise
½ tsp. pepper

Preheat oven to 400°.

1. Combine butter, parsley, breadcrumbs, salt and pepper, and spread over salmon slices. Place in a greased oven dish and bake for 15 minutes, basting frequently.

2. Remove and serve hot, with mayonnaise on the side.

Serves 4.

GRAVED LAKS (SWEDISH SALMON)

3 lb. fresh salmon (filet)   ½ Tbsp. red salt
1 tsp. salt   1 Tbsp. dill weed
½ Tbsp. sugar   1 Tbsp. salad oil
¼ Tbsp. fennel   1 Tbsp. brandy

Mix above items and spread over the salmon. Store in a cool place for 48 hours. To serve, slice salmon into very thin slices.

KOLOLE HALAKAHIKI SHRIMP

1 lb. raw shrimp
cooking oil

3 pinneapple slices,
canned

Sweet & Sour Sauce:
  ½ cup vinegar
  2 tsp. soya sauce
  4 Tbsp. pineapple juice
  ½ cup sugar
  1 Tbsp. cornstarch

Batter:
  ½ tsp. salt
  ½ cup flour
  2 eggs, lightly beaten

1. Clean shrimp and cut open back ridge of each to remove black veins. Wash and drain.

2. Mix sauce ingredients in saucepan. Bring to boil and simmer for about a minute, or until thick, stirring constantly. Remove from fire.

3. Combine batter ingredients and mix well to a smooth paste.

4. Dip shrimp into batter, coating well, and fry in hot oil until golden brown. Remove and place into Sweet & Sour Sauce.

5. Add 3 slices pineapple, cut into ½ in. pieces. Heat again over low flame and serve.

Serves 3 to 4.

SHRIMPS A LA PROVENCALE

1½ lbs. frozen shrimp,
  cooked
1 small can of peeled
  tomatoes
1 med. onion, finely
  chopped

½ lb. fresh mushrooms,
  sliced
touch of garlic
butter

Preheat oven to 350°.

1. Saute shrimp in butter for approximately 8 minutes, turning occasionally.

2. Chop onions finely, slice mushrooms, and saute together in pan. Add peeled tomatoes, touch of garlic, and simmer on low heat for 15 minutes.

3. Pour over shrimp and bake uncovered for 10 minutes.

Serve on bed of rice.

Serves 4.

This dish might also be called "Shrimps with Tomatoes and Garlic" for any dish labelled "provencale" means just that.

Tomatoes had a late start in food history. While they were mentioned in Greek writings as early as 200 A.D., they are believed to have originated in South America. In the 1500's, they were supposed to be both aphrodisiac and poisonous—an unlikely possibility.

The first tomato sauce was made in the Spanish royal court, and by 1850, tomato dishes were being prepared by the French.

Thomas Jefferson, in spite of the American belief that tomatoes produced sure death, enjoyed them regularly. It wasn't until after the Civil War that tomatoes lost their stigma and gained popular acceptance.

SOLE MEURNIERE

12 filets of Dover sole (2 lbs.)	chopped parsley
	touch of garlic
1 lemon	½ cup flour
¼ lb. butter	1 cup milk

1. Immerse filets in milk, then dip in flour. Heat butter in frying pan, medium heat. Cook filets in pan, slowly, for 8 minutes until golden brown, turning once. Remove from pan.

2. Add juice of lemon to same pan with touch of garlic. When hot, very quickly pour over filet in serving pan. Decorate with chopped parsley and lemon wedges.

Serves 4.

Note:
Haddock or pike may be substituted for sole.

SOLE DUGLERE

12 filets of sole
1 small onion, chopped
1 med. tomato, chopped
chopped parsley

¼ lb. butter
½ cup flour
1 cup milk
dash dry white wine

Preheat oven to 350°.

1. Melt butter in saucepan, add flour and then hot milk, stirring continuously. Simmer 7 minutes, medium heat.

2. Chop onion and tomato fine. Saute in small amount of butter in separate pan 7 minutes, then add cream sauce, salt and pepper to taste, and a dish of white wine if available. Add chopped parsley and simmer 3 minutes.

3. While sauce is cooking, place fish in baking dish. Sprinkle with butter and white wine. Bake 7 minutes.

4. Remove fish to serving platter and top with sauce.

Serves 4.

Note:
Adjust the number of filets according to size. Allow one large and one small filet per person. If the filets are all small, allow three per person.

DOVER SOLE MARGUERY

4 whole Dover sole
  (or 16 filet of sole)
touch of garlic
dash of salt, dash of
  fresh ground pepper
6 shallot onions, finely
  chopped

3 Tbsp. of butter
3 Tbsp. flour
3 cups of domestic dry
  chablis
1 cup heavy cream

Preheat oven to 350°.

1. Filet sole. It will yield 2 large and 2 small filets each. Serve 1 large and 1 small filet per person.

2. Put fishbones into a kettle with a bouquet of garlic, carrots, and celery. Cook down stock; after vegetables are fully cooked, reduce stock down until a good fish flavor has been obtained.

3. Make roux (butter and flour). Add stock gradually until a smooth sauce is obtained. Add cream. Cook well allowing no raw flour taste to remain. Set aside until needed.

4. Shortly before serving: In a buttered baking dish add shallot onions, touch of garlic, and poach filets carefully in a 350° oven. When done, remove filets to serving platter and keep hot. Reduce juices from poaching down to a third and add to strained sauce. Just before you serve, cover filets with sauce. Put under broiler and glaze. Serve immediately.

New parsley potatoes and any appropriate vegetable may accompany dish.

Serves 8.

NORWEGIAN HERRING SALAD

1 or 2 salted herring
  (enough to equal 1 cup)
½ cup of diced cooked
  beef (cold)
½ cup cold, cooked
  potatoes

1 cup diced pickled beets
½ cup diced raw apples
1 med. onion, diced
1 cup heavy mayonnaise
4 hard-boiled eggs
lettuce for garnish

(Salt herring may be found in small Scandanavian specialty food stores or larger supermarkets.)

1. Filet herring out and desalt in water overnight, changing water if necessary. Dry well and dice.

2. Add a touch of liquid from the beets to the mayonnaise to get desired color. Lightly toss all ingredients (except eggs and lettuce) together and chill until ready to use.

3. Separate egg white and yolk and chop both very fine. Use as a garnish on top of salad.

4. Serve the salad on chilled platter or individual plates, surrounded with crisp lettuce leaves.

Serves 3 to 4.

Buffalo certainly does not belong in our Foreign Favorites chapter since it was once a staple of American Indians, yet it is a foreign food to most of us. In the early 1800's more than ten million buffalo roamed the western plains. By 1900 only thirty buffalo remained in existence. The massive slaughter was supported by several groups who fancied themselves as leaders of progress. Removing the buffalo made railroad building easier and provided valuable hides. Fortunately, conservationists took those remaining thirty buffalo and protected them in the National Bison Range in Montana. Today there are over twenty-five thousand bison in protected, government and private herds.

To some, buffalo meat is more succulent than beef. If you're lucky enough to find a supply of buffalo meat, try this recipe or use any recipe calling for beef.

SWEETGRASS BUFFALO AND BEER PIE

4 lbs. buffalo meat
salt, pepper, sage, oil,
  flour
3 med. onions
3 carrots
3 stalks celery
3 potatoes
3 Tbsp. flour

2 pts. beef stock
2 Tbsp. tomato puree
1 pt. beer
herb bag containing a garlic
  clove, a bay leaf, parsley,
  3 cloves, a pinch of thyme
1 pastry stick
milk

1. Cut meat in 1 in. cubes, season with salt, pepper and sage, roll in flour and brown in oil.

2. Transfer meat to a heavy saucepan.

3. Cut vegetables in ½ in. cubes, saute in the same oil and add to the meat.

4. Add 3 Tbsp. flour to the oil and let it brown.

5. Add stock, tomato puree and beer and blend; add herb bag, add all the meat and vegetables and simmer until tender.

6. Remove the herb bag; place stew in a casserole or individual pot pie oven dishes, cover with pastry, brush with milk.

7. Bake in 400° oven until golden brown.

Serves 6 to 8.

Nothing in food history seems more important than bread. It is so basic to human life that it has become a synonym—breadwinner for the head of house, bread meaning money in current slang, bread meaning any kind of nourishment, as in Deuteronomy 8:4, "man doth not live by bread only."

Pieces of bread were used to hold food before dishes became common. The Greeks used bread to clean up food juices the way we use napkins. The Egyptians made bread back in 4000 B.C. Few foods have achieved bread's level of importance and maintained it for nearly 6,000 years.

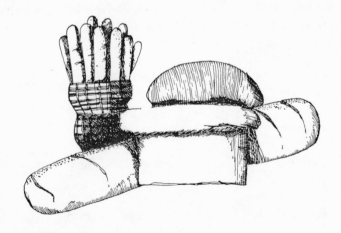

IRISH SODA BREAD

4½ lbs. flour	1 Tbsp. salt
6 Tbsp. shortening	4 Tbsp. baking powder
6 Tbsp. sugar	1 Tbsp. soda
1 qt. buttermilk	1 pt. water

Preheat oven to 400°.

1. Mix flour, salt, baking powder, sugar, and soda thoroughly. When thoroughly mixed, cut in shortening, add buttermilk and water.

2. Knead it together and divide into 5 loaves of 1 lb. 12 oz. each. Mold in 9 in. round cake pans.

3. Brush with buttermilk and sprinkle sugar on top of it. Bake for 45 minutes.

Yield:
5 loaves

Variation:
With raisins, same as above only add 10 oz. raisins.

Chef's Tip:
Cut loaves across top with a large "X" before baking to make traditional soda bread shape.

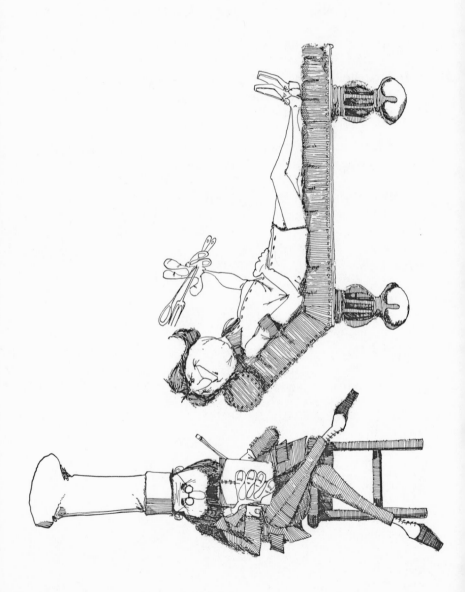

Chapter 7

Mixed Up Dishes

Casseroles by any other name are still mixed up dishes. Here are a few easy ones that are suprisingly good.

RICE CASSEROLE

1 cup uncooked rice
  (reconstituted)
2 cans beef consumme
1 or 2 small cans of sliced
  mushrooms, drained

2 Tbsp. minced onion
1 tsp. curry
4 strips of crisp bacon
1 small package of slivered
  almonds

Preheat oven to 400°.

1. Put all ingredients except almonds in heavy, buttered casserole. Cover.

2. Bake in oven at 400° for 1 hour.

3. Remove from oven and add almonds. Mix well and serve hot.

Serves 4.

Rice was first used by the Chinese from 2500 to 5000 years ago depending upon which historian you support. In the 6th century B.C., according to legend, Buddha lived for a while on one grain of rice per day. A contemporary of his, Confucius, also valued rice highly and it soon became a part of Chinese philosophy. As Buddhism spread throughout the Orient, so did the importance of rice.

According to Oriental tradition, the best rice is harvested by the hands of women. Considering rice harvesting takes six hundred to a thousand hours per acre, that's a lot of "women's work" just to satisfy tradition!

BRUNCH CHEESE CASSEROLE

3 slices white bread
½ lb. American or Ched-
   dar cheese, shredded
4 eggs

1 tsp. salt
1 tsp. mustard
2 cups milk
paprika

1. Butter casserole heavily.

2. Cut crusts off the bread and cut into 1 in. square pieces. Place bread in the bottom of casserole and sprinkle shredded cheese over the top. (Shredded package cheese is advisable.)

3. Beat eggs and add the salt, mustard and milk. Pour mixture over the bread and cheese. Sprinkle with paprika generously.

4. Refrigerate for a minimum of 12 hours. Remove from refrigerator 45 minutes before baking. Bake 1 hour at 325° in an uncovered casserole.

This casserole can be reheated without losing any of its texture or taste.

Serves 6.

CHEF JOHN'S SEAFOOD CASSEROLE

1 small can crabmeat
1 small can shrimp
½ pt. oysters, fresh
  (shucked) or canned
⅔ cup dry breadcrumbs
⅔ cup grated sharp cheese
6 Tbsp. butter

3 Tbsp. flour
1½ cups milk
¼ tsp. dry mustard
1 tsp. Worcestershire
  sauce
salt and pepper
dash nutmeg or mace

Preheat oven to 400°.

1. Melt the butter. Add flour, milk and seasonings. Mix, cook, and stir until thickened. Add the seafood.

2. Pour into a buttered casserole. Sprinkle with breadcrumbs. Bake for 15 minutes.

3. Top with the cheese. Continue baking for 5 to 10 minutes before serving.

Serves 4.

SAVOURY MEAT LOAF

3 lbs. ground beef
½ cup finely chopped celery
½ cup finely chopped onion
½ cup chopped mushrooms

2 tsp. chopped parsley
1 roll of pastry
2 eggs, beaten
6 strips bacon
1 Tbsp. Worcestershire sauce

Preheat oven to 350°.

1. Saute onions, mushrooms and celery in pan until cooked. Combine in a bowl with the beef. Add beaten egg, parsley, Worcestershire sauce, salt and pepper.

2. Roll out pastry in shape large enough to cover loaf. Shape meat into a loaf, and place on pastry. Lay strips of bacon around the meat and fold pastry over loaf to cover.

3. Bake for 1 hour. Cut into slices. This meat loaf can be served either hot or cold.

Serves 6 to 8.

Chef's Tip:
For a shiny glaze, beat 1 egg and brush over the pastry before baking the loaf.

MACARONI AND TUNA

2 cups elbow macaroni
12 oz. canned tuna fish
½ cup butter
½ cup flour
2 Tbsp. chopped onions

3½ cups milk
1 Tbsp. salt
3 Tbsp. grated cheese,
   Parmesan or Cheddar
dash of nutmeg

Preheat oven to 350°.

1. Drop macaroni into 3 cups rapidly boiling salted water. Bring to a boil again, stirring occasionally. Cook for 6 or 7 minutes and then drain and place in casserole.

2. Mix flaked tuna with macaroni.

3. Saute chopped onions in butter in a saucepan, adding the flour. Stir and add milk, salt and nutmeg. Bring to a boil and add 2 Tbsp. of the grated cheese. Pour over macaroni and tuna.

4. Sprinkle remaining cheese over the top of the casserole and bake for 40 minutes.

Serves 6.

SAUERKRAUT HOT DISH

1 qt. sauerkraut (No. 2 can, drain and reserve liquid)
1 cup uncooked rice

1 lb. hamburger
½ lb. pork sausage
3 slices bacon

1. Cook rice until done.

2. Make small meatballs of the hamburger and sausage. Brown in a frying pan.

3. Combine the rice and sauerkraut, fold in the meatballs carefully so as not to crumble.

4. Place in a 2 qt. casserole, be sure there is enough juice from the kraut in this mixture. (Approximately 1 inch of liquid is desirable; water may be added.)

5. Top with raw bacon and bake for 30 minutes at 375°.

Serves 4.

Would you believe the Chinese invented sauerkraut? It seems that back around 200 B.C., they pickled cabbage in wine to preserve it. Then good old Genghis Khan in 1200 A.D. replaced the wine with salt. His Mongol tribes carried their salted cabbage with them to eastern Europe where eventually the Germans adopted it and called it "sauerkraut" (sour plant).

PAULINE'S CURRIED WILD RICE
CASSEROLE

1 cup cooked wild rice
½ cup cooked shrimp,
  crabmeat or tuna
  (or combination of
  shrimp and crabmeat)
½ cup sauteed mushrooms
  (small, whole)
2 Tbsp. green pepper,
  chopped

2 Tbsp. pimentoes or
  pimento stuffed olives,
  chopped
2 hard-boiled eggs (dice
  whites and reserve yolks)
1 can cream of mushroom
  soup
1 tsp. curry powder
¼ cup sliced salted almonds

Preheat oven to 350°.

1. Mix all ingredients together (except almonds and egg
   yolks). Put in small, buttered baking dish, sprinkle
   with almonds, cover and bake 30 minutes.

2. Before serving, garnish by sprinkling with crumbled
   egg yolks.

Serves 4.

HOT DISH A LA JANE

1 lb. ground beef
½ stalk celery, diced
1 green pepper, chopped
2 med. onions, chopped
1 can tomato soup,
  undiluted
1 can cream of mushroom
  soup, undiluted

¼ tsp. garlic salt
¼ tsp. Worcestershire
  sauce
1 small pkg. thin noodles,
  cooked
¼ lb. grated Colby
  cheese (or Cheddar)

Preheat oven to 350°.

1. Brown meat and saute celery, pepper and onions in small amount of cooking oil. Cover and simmer until green pepper is tender.

2. Stir in both soups, cooked noodles, garlic salt and Worcestershire sauce. Transfer to casserole. Sprinkle with grated cheese and bake until cheese is crusty (approximately 15 minutes).

Serves 4.

Chapter 8

Vegetables Can Be Beautiful...
So Can Fruits

Perhaps no other foods are as maligned as vegetables. Little boys push them aside. Big ones stoically endure them. But contrary to popular belief, vegetables can be beautiful! Delicious, too. From the lowly potato to the lofty artichoke, here are some elegant ways with vegetables, and a few fruits as well!

FRENCH PEAS IN A BASKET

1 stick pie crust dough (or 1 recipe of pie crust)
8-4 in. aluminum foil cups

2-No. 2 cans of sweet peas, drained
1 small jar mint jelly
¾ cup onions, chopped fine

Preheat oven to 325º.

1. Roll out dough and cut to line foil cups. Place a weighted empty foil cup on top of the dough to retain shape while baking. Bake until brown, approximately 25 to 40 minutes.

2. Fill each cup with a portion of peas topped with 2 Tbsp. mint jelly and 1 Tbsp. chopped onion.

Serves 8.

PIMENTO CUPS WITH ARTICHOKE HEARTS

6 whole canned
  pimentos
1½ cups finely minced
  celery
3 anchovies, chopped
2 Tbsp. finely minced
  onion
⅓ cup mayonnaise

½ tsp. salt
⅛ tsp. pepper
6 cooked artichoke
  hearts or bottoms
garlic flavored French
  dressing
crisp greens

1. Drain pimentos.

2. Combine celery, anchovies, onion and enough mayonnaise to bind the other ingredients. Season with salt and pepper.

3. Fill pimento cups with the celery-anchovy mixture, and top with an artichoke heart or bottom that has been marinated in the garlic flavored French dressing. Arrange on individual plates garnished with crisp greens.

Serves 6.

If vegetables are not the most popular food in your household, take comfort in the knowledge that it may be based on an attitude that has been nurtured for centuries. The early English ate few vegetables, nothing much more than radishes, spinach, cabbage and lettuce. Dried peas were turned into porridge—"pease porridge hot, pease porridge cold, pease porridge in the pot nine days old." Green peas were not commonly eaten until the 18th century.

Other Europeans cultivated and consumed more vegetables than the English, but were slow to accept new varieties. The colonists brought their eating habits to America and nearly starved before realizing the importance of vegetables. The new world provided new adventures in vegetable eating with corn, pimento (or pimiento), potatoes, pumpkins, sweet potatoes, string beans, peppers and more.

CASSEROLE OF BRUSSELS SPROUTS
(Ledbury Style)

2 lbs. Brussels sprouts
4 cups hot milk
¾ cup flour
1 cup melted butter
1 cup Cheddar or Parmesan cheese, grated

2 tsp. Worcestershire sauce
pinch of nutmeg
salt and pepper
paprika

Preheat oven to 350°.

1. Cook washed and trimmed sprouts in boiling salted water until they are tender (approximately 15 to 20 minutes). When cooked, drain well.

2. Heat melted butter in pan. Add flour, stirring constantly. The add hot milk, stirring until it thickens. Add cheese and Worcestershire sauce, pinch of nutmeg and season to taste.

3. Saute Brussels sprouts in butter. Add sauce. Put in casserole dish, sprinkle with additional cheese and paprika. Bake for 20 minutes.

Serves 6 to 8.

LENTEN CABBAGE

1 med. head of cabbage
1 lb. fish filets, roughly
   chopped (salmon, pike,
   halibut)
½ cup cooked rice

½ cup chopped onion
1 egg
½ tsp. salt
½ tsp. pepper
dash nutmeg

Preheat oven to 350°.

1. Core cabbage. Cook for 5 minutes in boiling water. Cool under running water and drain. Divide outer leaves into 4 servings.

2. Mix egg with fish, rice, onion and seasonings. Chop center of cabbage and add to mixture.

3. Divide into 4 portions and place in center of the cabbage leaves. Fold opposite corners across stuffing and place open side down in buttered baking dish. Add about ¼ cup water and bake covered for 20 minutes and then bake 15 minutes uncovered.

Serves 4.

Chef's Tip:
Be sure to completely remove cabbage core before boiling. Use the remaining liquid in casserole for sauce.

During the reign of Elizabeth I, royal law forbade the serving of meat during Lent. Innkeepers could serve only fish. Religion had little to do with the law that also forbade serving meat on Fridays throughout the year. The "fish days" were established by the Crown to encourage the fisherman who also served in Britain's powerful navy. During the 16th century, without a happy navy, Britain could not have ruled the waves and maintained economic stability at home.

SPINACH RING

2½ cups chopped spinach	1 tsp. grated onion
1 cup milk	1 Tbsp. lemon juice
3 Tbsp. butter	2 eggs, well-beaten
3 Tbsp. flour	1 tsp. salt
⅓ tsp. nutmeg	

Preheat oven to 375°.

1. Mix all ingredients together and pour into a well-buttered ring mold. Place in a hot water bath, taking care that water does not come over ring, but comes just to top of mold. Bake until firm, approximately 30 minutes, until spinach springs back at touch.

2. Unmold on a hot, round tray or plate, and fill the center with a creamed vegetable, creamed seafood or chicken. Or make into individual molds and fill with creamed chicken (cut 1 in. cubes), shrimp or lobster and serve as a luncheon entree.

Serves 6.

BAKED STUFFED POTATOES

3 large baking potatoes
6 tsp. chopped chives
6 tsp. crumbled crisp
   bacon (6 strips)
½ cup sour cream

1 finely chopped onion
1 egg yolk
1 Tbsp. melted butter
paprika

Preheat oven to 350°.

1. Bake potatoes until tender.

2. When tender, cut in half. Scoop out potato into a bowl and whip. Reserve shells.

3. Combine chives, onion, bacon, beaten egg yolk and sour cream.

4. Stir into whipped potato.

5. Spoon mixture back into potato shell. Sprinkle with paprika and melted butter.

6. Bake at 350° for 15 minutes.

Serves 6.

Potatoes were introduced to Europe by the Spanish conquistadors who found them in South America in the mid-1500's. Ireland, often credited with the origin of the potato, began growing them in the 18th century. Our word "spud" comes from the Irish method of planting potatoes with a spade. The French were the last of the Europeans to accept potatoes, which they thought produced leprosy. In fact, a French agriculturist-botanist included potatoes on a list of items with horsechestnuts and acorns to be eaten only in case of famine.

HOME HASHED BROWNED POTATOES

2 tsp. butter, melted	1½ tsp. salt
2 tsp. fat	⅛ tsp. pepper
4 med. potatoes	

1. Boil the potatoes and remove from water just before you normally would consider done. Peel potatoes and grate on large size grater.

2. Melt fat in heavy skillet. Mix grated potatoes with butter and seasonings, and brown in the hot fat over low heat. Turn potatoes with a spatula after about 5 minutes and let brown on the other side.

Serves 4.

Chef's Tip:
Cool or chill potatoes before grating.

GERMAN POTATO SALAD

4 large potatoes (2 lbs.)	salt and pepper
3 oz. onion	4 oz. bacon
2 Tbsp. vinegar	

1. Cook potatoes until done. Peel and dice potatoes.

2. Dice bacon and place in a fry pan, saute until lightly brown.

3. Add warm potatoes, vinegar, salt and pepper. Mix with a large wooden spoon. If too dry, add a little cream and mix again.

Serves 8.

BAKED PINEAPPLE SWEET POTATOES

1 med. can sweet
   potatoes, mashed
½ tsp. salt
1-No. 2 can crushed
   pineapple, drained

½ cup brown sugar
¼ lb. butter or margarine
marshmallows (small)

Preheat oven to 350°.

1. Mix potatoes with salt and put half of mixture in a 9 in. round buttered casserole. Add layer of pineapple, then remaining half of potatoes. Top with brown sugar, dot with butter and cover with marshmallows.

2. Bake uncovered until marshmallows are light brown, (approximately 15 minutes).

Serves 4.

No doubt this next piece of information alone will be worth the price of this book. Marshmallows no longer contain marshmallow!

A mallow is a plant related to hollyhocks and the roots of marshmallows produce a sticky juice. This juice was once the basis for our well-known marshmallow confection. It has since been replaced by gelatin, so there is no longer marshmallow juice in marshmallows.

Appalling!

MEDITERRANEAN GREEN GODDESS SALAD

1 head of lettuce
½ cup feta cheese (goat cheese), crumbled
8 slices tomato
Green Goddess dressing
½ cup spinach (fresh)

1 cup croutons
Mid-East spices (to taste)
Parmesan cheese
½ cup shrimp
4 anchovies (sliced)
1 clove garlic

1. Break lettuce into bite-size pieces.

2. In a large bowl that has been rubbed with garlic, toss above ingredients, except tomatoes and Parmesan cheese. Add one at a time mixing well each time. Add dressing last, and use it sparingly.

3. Place on individual serving plates and garnish with tomato slices and Parmesan cheese, to taste.

Serves 4.

Chef's tip for lettuce preparation:

1. Remove outside protective leaves.

2. Rap core of lettuce sharply on table and remove from head.

3. Wash lettuce in cold water, running water into the hole left by the core. Shake dry, leaving a few beads of water on to help retain some moisture. DO NOT drown the lettuce in water.

4. Place in refrigerator, very well-covered with a damp cloth until needed.

SALADE KATHRYN MARY

2 pkg. quick frozen artichoke hearts
2 med. heads of lettuce, shredded
2 cups raw cauliflorets
2 large tomatoes, diced
2 Tbsp. chopped chives
2 large ripe olives, sliced
4 large stuffed green olives, sliced
¼ cup chopped dill pickle
French salad dressing

1. Cook artichoke hearts as directed on pkg. Rinse with cold water and cut each heart in half. Chill.

2. Prepare remaining ingredients, keeping each separate. Lightly toss together lettuce, half of the cauliflower, half the tomato, and all the chives in a large salad bowl. Arrange remaining ingredients in vertical rows over top of salad.

For an especially attractive pattern, arrange a row of artichokes around edge and down middle of bowl. On each side of the center row of artichokes, place a row of olives and pickles, one of remaining cauliflower and one of remaining tomato. To serve, sprinkle dressing across half of bowl and toss lightly. Serve from that section keeping the rest of the design intact until the first part is finished.

Serves 12.

MOM'S AVOCADO SALAD

2 ripe avocados
2 Tbsp. lemon juice
1 cup flaked crabmeat
2 eggs, hard-boiled,
  diced
dash of white pepper
¼ cup water chestnuts,
  chopped

½ tsp. Worcestershire
  sauce
¼ cup chopped ripe
  olives
¼ cup cashew nuts,
  chopped
½ cup mayonnaise

1. Halve avocados and remove the seed. Scoop out the meat and sprinkle the meat and shell with lemon juice. Dice the avocado meat.

2. Combine olives and cashews with mayonnaise. Mix with crabmeat, chopped water chestnuts, diced avocado meat and hard-boiled eggs.

3. Season to taste with salt, white pepper, lemon juice and Worcestershire sauce.

4. Mound the mixture on top of avocado halves and garnish plate with sliced tomato, sliced hard-boiled eggs, grapes, lemon wedge and parsley on large lettuce leaf. Serve with blue cheese dressing.

Serves 2 to 4.

CALIFORNIA SALAD

1 avocado, peeled and
   diced
1 tomato, peeled and
   diced
½ bell pepper, sliced
   thin
small bunch of green
   onions, diced (save white
   part for dressing)

½ head of lettuce,
   sliced thin
½ peeled cucumber,
   diced
2 tsp. grated Parmesan
   cheese

DRESSING

¼ cup green onion, diced
¼ cup salad vinegar
¼ cup salad oil
½ tsp. salt
¼ tsp. ground pepper
1 tsp. sugar

2 crushed garlic cloves
1 pinch oregano
1 pinch thyme
1 raw egg (add just
   before serving)

1. Mix the above dressing in a small glass jar. Chill. Add the raw egg just before serving. Shake jar until dressing becomes smooth. You can substitute 3 tsp. of mayonnaise for the raw egg.

2. Mix salad in a bowl and pour the dressing over. Sprinkle with more Parmesan cheese to taste.

Serves 4.

SALAD NICOISE

1 small can tuna fish
2 doz. anchovie filets
½ cup stuffed olives
   (med. size whole)
2 heads Boston lettuce
2 ripe tomatoes

2 med. green peppers
1 small red onion
1 cup olive oil
1 cup white wine vinegar
salt and pepper to taste

1. Desalt anchovies by running cool water over them. Chill.

2. Clean lettuce and drain very dry.

3. Remove skins from tomatoes by blanching in hot water. Cut tomatoes into six pieces each.

4. Cut seeds from green pepper and cut into julienne strips.

5. Slice onions very thin.

6. Cover vegetables and chill until ready to serve.

7. Drain tuna fish and chill.

8. Just before serving, place all ingredients into a chilled bowl and toss very carefully with the dressing made from the oil, vinegar, salt and pepper.

Serves 4 to 6.

BOUQUET OF FRUIT A LA ALICE

¼ fresh pineapple, sliced
4 grapefruit sections
6 orange sections
3 melon sections
6 apple slices

1 scoop cottage cheese
1 small Jello mold
1 small bunch of grapes
1 leaf of lettuce
strawberries as garnish

Place leaf lettuce on chilled dinner plate and arrange all other items attractively on it.

Some fruits are picked before maturity and can be ripened at home at room temperature—bananas, pears, peaches, pineapple, plums and some melons. Not, however, watermelons. They must ripen on the vine. Grapes, cherries, blueberries, strawberries, citrus fruits and apples must also be ripe before picking as they will not ripen further after harvesting. Store all ripe fruit except bananas in a cool place.

Chapter 9

Doggie Bag Variations

What to do with leftovers plagues every homemaker and chef alike. Whether they came home in a doggie bag from your favorite restaurant or are simply the over supply from last night's meal, those leftovers need help. Here are a few ways to turn leftovers into family favorites.

IRISH POTATO BREAD

2 cups mashed potatoes   2 tsp. baking powder
2 Tbsp. flour   3 tsp. bacon fat, melted
¼ tsp. salt

1. Mix flour, salt and baking powder together. Add to potatoes. Add melted fat and mix well.

2. Form 16 patties and bake on greased grill, turning over—until golden brown.

Serve hot with butter.

Serves 4 to 6.

POTATO MUFFINS

1 cup mashed potatoes, hot
½ cup milk
1 egg, beaten
1 cup flour
1 tsp. salt
1 Tbsp. melted butter
2 tsp. baking powder
¼ cup sugar

Preheat oven to 400°.

1. Sprinkle melted butter on mashed potatoes.

2. Sift dry ingredients and mix with potatoes.

3. Stir in milk by degrees, add beaten egg.

4. Fill greased muffin tins ¾ full.

Bake 25 minutes in a 400° oven.

Serves 8.

HAM AND CHEESE SALAD

12 oz. ham, diced
10 oz. cheese, diced
1 med. onion, diced
4 Tbsp. vinegar
3 Tbsp. salad oil
2 Tbsp. water
1 or 2 dill pickles, diced

1. Place all ingredients in a salad bowl and toss until well mixed.

2. Place in refrigerator until served.

Serves 4.

Chef's Tip:
Serve a dark bread with above salad.

POLONESIAN KABAB

5 oz. ham, cut in 5 cubes   1 slice pineapple,
1 cooked sweet potato,   cut in 4
   cut in 4   cinnamon

Preheat broiler.

1. On skewer, place alternate pieces of ham, sweet potato and pineapple, beginning and ending with ham.

2. Broil to a golden brown. Sprinkle with cinnamon.

Serve on bed of stewed corn and diced tomato with cider sauce.

Serves 1.

Chef's Tip:
Orange slices, prunes or dates may be substituted for pineapple.
Cider sauce: Cider thickened with cornstarch.

TURKEY OF THE RITZ

2 slices of turkey breast,
 cooked
1 slice of white bread,
 toasted
3 slices of tomato
2 slices of bacon,
 crisply fried

½ cup supreme sauce
sprig of parsley
spiced peach half
slivered almonds

1. Place tomato slices on top of the toasted slice of bread. Cover with turkey slices and supreme sauce. Add the crisply fried bacon crosswise over the sauce and sprinkle the slivered almonds over all.

2. Garnish with spiced peach half, spiced apple or apple rings.

Serves 1.

Chef's Tip:
Supreme sauce is simply white sauce made with cream and chicken stock instead of milk. For one cup sauce, use ⅓ cup cream and ⅔ cup chicken stock.

It is possible to serve turkey without having some left over? We think not, so you'll find a number of recipes here using cooked turkey. Frozen turkey rolls can also be substituted for the leftover variety.

This whole turkey business started with the discovery of the Americas. By the time the Pilgrims had Thanksgiving dinner, turkeys had already been introduced into Spain by the Spanish explorers returning from their new world expeditions.

Benjamin Franklin was so taken with the turkey that he felt it should have been our national bird instead of the bald eagle. That might have eliminated the need for leftover turkey recipes.

TURKEY TETRAZZINI

1 Tbsp. butter
flour to thicken
¼ cup diced onion
small clove garlic, diced
pinch of oregano
1½ cup cubed leftover turkey, preferably dark meat
1 cup chicken stock, warm
2 Tbsp. diced pimento
¼ cup stuffed olives, sliced

¼ cup sliced canned mushrooms
3 oz. spaghetti or noodles, cut into 2 in. pieces, cooked and drained
salt and pepper to taste
Parmesan cheese, grated
4 Tbsp. shredded Cheddar cheese

Preheat oven to 450º.

1. Melt butter in fry pan, add onion, garlic and oregano. Saute until golden, add turkey. When bubbling, sprinkle with enough flour to absorb all the butter, then add the warm chicken stock, stir until smooth.

2 Add pimentos, canned mushrooms and olives. Season with salt and pepper.

3. Now add the drained spaghetti. Stir gently.

4. Remove from heat and pour into casserole dish, sprinkle with Parmesan cheese, cover with shredded Cheddar cheese. Brown in very hot oven or under broiler.

Serves 4 to 6.

TURKEY PASTIE

1 lb. cubed turkey, white and dark meat
1 med. onion, diced
1 cup frozen peas and carrots
½ cup sliced canned mushrooms
2 oz. butter and flour to thicken
dash of thyme
salt and pepper to taste
1¼ cup stock (Bring 1 chicken boullion cube to a boil in 1½ cups of milk. Let simmer 5 minutes.)*
1 raw egg, beaten with 1 Tbsp. milk

Use your favorite pastry or puff paste dough, rolled thin and cut round about the size of a dinner plate. Roll out 6 circles.

Preheat oven to 375°.

1. Melt butter in deep pan, add onion and thyme. Saute until onion turns transparent. Add flour and stir until all the butter has been absorbed, then add stock, turn down heat and let simmer 2 to 3 minutes. Add frozen vegetables, mushrooms, and turkey. When this comes to a boil, remove from heat and allow to cool.

2. Brush pastry dough with egg and milk batter. Place a serving of turkey mixture (amount preferred) a bit off-center on the dough. Fold over pastry dough and seal edges. Brush again with egg-milk mixture. This prevents pastry from burning and makes it more crisp. Seal the pastie by pressing a fork down on the seam. This gives a laced appearance and makes it very appetizing.

3. Bake on a cookie sheet 20 to 30 minutes or until brown.

* 1¼ to 1½ cups of giblet gravy may be used instead of chicken stock.

Serves 4 to 6.

TURKEY SHORTCAKE

4 corn muffins
8 good slices turkey
 breast
12 pieces cooked asparagus
4 slices cooked ham

½ cup flour
½ cup butter
2½ cups chicken stock
2 tomatoes, halved
 and broiled

Preheat oven to 350°.

1. Melt butter in saucepan. Mix flour into butter. Add 2 cups chicken stock, stirring constantly and well. Cook for 10 minutes on low heat.

2. Heat in oven the ham, turkey and asparagus in a casserole with ½ cup stock. At the same time, warm the corn muffins in the oven.

3. Break corn muffins in half and place on the plates. Alternate ham and turkey on top of muffins. Cover with the hot cream sauce.

Garnish plate with asparagus and ½ broiled tomato.

Serves 4.

SAVORY BROCCOLI TURKEY DIVINE

2 cups croutons
2 Tbsp. butter, melted
1 cup white sauce
12 pieces broccoli spears
10 oz. sliced turkey
fine herbs (parsley or
   thyme, and nutmeg)

¾ cup butter
2 egg yolks
1 Tbsp. lemon juice
2 Tbsp. whipped cream
¼ cup Parmesan cheese
dash red pepper (cayenne)

Preheat oven to 375°.

1. Place croutons on baking sheet. Pour butter over evenly. Sprinkle with herbs. Mix lightly to absorb butter. Place in oven until golden brown.

2. Use 4 individual sized casseroles. Place ½ cup croutons on bottom of each casserole. Ladle 2 Tbsp. of white sauce over croutons. Arrange 3 pieces broccoli over the croutons and sauce. Top above with 2 oz. turkey and 2 Tbsp. of white sauce. Sprinkle each casserole with 1 Tbsp. of cheese.

3. Blend half of the butter, eggs, and lemon juice in double boiler over water. Stir constantly until butter is melted. Mix in remaining butter and stir until thickened. Remove from flame, add whipped cream. Stir seasonings into above. Spoon 2 Tbsp. of sauce over each serving. Place under broiler until golden brown. Serve garnished with parsley.

Serves 4.

MINNEAPOLITAN SANDWICH

4 slices turkey
2 slices of toast
2 slices bacon, partially
   fried

2 mushroom caps
1 cup cheese sauce*

Preheat oven to 400°.

*Cheese Sauce: Add ½ cup nippy Cheddar cheese to 1 cup white sauce. Add Worcestershire to taste. Cook until blended.

1. In casserole place 2 slices trimmed toast, add turkey, top with cheese sauce. Place partially fried bacon on cheese sauce and garnish with mushrooms.

2. Place in oven for about 5 minutes, or until cheese sauce browns.

Serves 1.

TURKEY SALAD WITH DICED PINEAPPLE

1 lb. diced turkey (white
  and dark meat)
3 pineapple slices, diced
  or chunks
6 asparagus spears, diced
6 mushrooms, sliced into
  quarters

1½ cups mayonnaise
3 Tbsp. tomato catsup
1 tsp. horseradish
1 tsp. salt
pineapple juice as
  required

1. Add catsup, horseradish and pineapple juice to the
   mayonnaise (adjusting the amount of juice to reach a
   thin sauce consistency). Mix well.

2. Add turkey and remaining ingredients to the sauce.
   Chill.

Serve in salad bowls with lettuce leaf garnish.

Serves 4.

TURKEY SALAD BOMBAY

1 cup of mayonnaise
½ cup of sour cream
3 Tbsp. of curry powder
¼ cup of chutney,
  chopped fine
2 cups of cooked turkey
  leftovers, cubed

¼ cup of salted peanuts
1 cup of partially cooked
  apples (unpeeled), cubed
2 cups of cooked rice

1. Blend mayonnaise, sour cream and curry powder in blender.

2. Toss remaining ingredients and fold in mayonnaise mixture.

3. Serve on lettuce cups and garnish with toasted coconut.

Serves 4.

Chutney, so often used in and with curried dishes is an Indian condiment made from Malaga raisins, mangoes, apples, brown sugar, vinegar, lemon peel, garlic and ginger.

In place of the usual salted peanuts called for in the above recipe, try salted-in-the-shell peanuts. Rather than the more traditional shelling, roasting in oil and salting process, these peanuts undergo a brine bath and are then roasted, shell and all. The salted-in-the-shell peanut is an American improvement on an old French process. Its first commercial production was in the 1920's by Samuel S. Fisher in St. Paul, Minnesota. The founder of the Fisher Nut Company, Mr. Fisher had watched French peasants soak raw peanuts in salt water and then dry them in the sun. He liked the salty flavor but felt the nut should be more crunchy. So he developed the salted-in-the-shell roasting method now used by commercial peanut processors.

JANE'S FAVORITE CHICKEN SALAD

4 cups cooked chicken, cubed
1 cup celery, diced
1 cup seedless green grapes (canned or fresh)
1 tsp. salt
¼ tsp. pepper

1 cup toasted slivered almonds (or sunflower nuts)
¾ cup mayonnaise
¼ cup sour cream
4 lettuce leaves

1. Combine chicken, celery, grapes, salt, pepper and nuts in mixing bowl.

2. Stir in mayonnaise and sour cream and mix thoroughly. Chill and serve on lettuce leaves.

Serves 4.

Chapter 10

Appetite Appeasers

In ancient Rome, it was customary to visit friends in the late afternoon and enjoy a glass of wine. While guests were polite enough to bring their own wine, the host would always provide plenty of tasty "appetite appeasers," forerunners to our modern day appetizers. Serve any of these next time friends drop in, even if they don't bring their own wine.

GUACAMOLE

2 avocados, peeled,
  seeded and sliced
4 Tbsp. olive oil
1 Tbsp. chives or
  green onion tops

1 tsp. dill weed
2 Tbsp. lemon juice
1 clove of garlic
1 tsp. salt
dash of hot pepper sauce

1. Place all ingredients in blender. Cover and blend on high speed until smooth, stopping to stir down if necessary.

2. Store in refrigerator until ready to serve.

3. Dip with potato chips, crackers, toast or raw cauliflower.

Makes about 1½ cups dip.

JANE'S TOASTIES

6 oz. can tuna or crabmeat, drained and flaked

3 Tbsp. chopped sunflower nuts

3 English muffins

few drops lemon juice

2 Tbsp. chopped onion

2 Tbsp. butter or salad dressing

6 slices processed cheese, cut in quarters

4 slices bacon, fried and crumbled

1. Combine fish, onion and sunflower nuts. Moisten with butter or salad dressing. Add lemon juice.

2. Split muffins in half. Butter halves, then cut each half in quarters and spread with fish mixture.

3. Top each with crumbled bacon and pieces of cheese.

4. Broil 3 to 4 minutes or until cheese is melted. Serve warm.

Makes 24 bite-sized delicacies.

For heartier appetites, leave muffin halves whole and top with whole cheese slices.

The earliest cocktail parties may have been the ancient Egyptians' preludes to feasting. Pickled onions and various seeds—anise, curmin and sesame—were nibbled while guests sipped liquid refreshments and watched dancing girls perform. They also ate green cabbage leaves which they thought delayed drunkenness.

Early Greeks ate roasted grasshoppers, caviar, cheeses, oysters, olives, shrimp and pistachio nuts as "provocatives to drinking."

COQUILLES SAINT-JACQUES

1 pt. dry white wine
2 lbs. of scallops
½ lb. mushrooms
6 shallots
1 Tbsp. parsley
1 Tbsp. lemon juice
2 Tbsp. water

2 Tbsp. butter
2 egg yolks
sharp cheese, grated
4 Tbsp. cream
salt, pepper, and
   monosodium glutamate
   to taste

1. Bring wine to boil, add scallops and simmer 5 minutes. Drain and save wine.

2. Simmer shallots, parsley, lemon juice, water, salt, pepper, monosodium glutamate, and mushrooms in butter until done.

3. Make roux of flour and butter. Add wine and simmer, stirring until thick.

4. Cut scallops in quarters and add to sauce. Add rest of cooked ingredients to sauce. Add egg yolks and cream. Mix well, but do not boil.

5. Dish into shells and sprinkle with sharp cheese. Place in oven or broiler until bubbling, then serve.

Serves 6.

SHRIMP COCKTAIL SAUCE

1 cup mayonnaise
½ cup ketchup
¼ cup light cream
1 tsp. horseradish
few drops lemon juice

dash of red pepper
1 Tbsp. brandy (optional)
1 lb. small shrimp
⅓ head of lettuce

1. Cook, cool and peel shrimp.*

2. Shred lettuce and place in cocktail dish until half full.

3. Mix mayonnaise and ketchup until smooth. Add remaining ingredients in above order.

4. Use about 6 shrimp for each serving. Put shrimp on top of the shredded lettuce and cover with the sauce.

Serves 6.

Chef's Tip:
This sauce also makes a tasty salad dressing. The brandy adds a special zest to the sauce when used with shrimp.

*Shrimp should be cooked in: 1 qt. water, 1 Tbsp. vinegar, 1 stalk celery, 1 carrot, 1 onion, 1 tsp. caraway seed, and 1 Tbsp. salt. Bring above ingredients to a boil. Add shrimp and boil 3 minutes. Remove from heat and let stand 10 minutes. Drain, peel, devein and cool.

CANAPE LOAF

Preheat oven to 400º.

1. Round edges of a loaf of unsliced white bread.

2. Hollow out top of loaf. Brush outside of loaf with oil.

3. Brown in 400º oven.

4. Cool and decorate with cheese squares, cocktail sausages, cooked shrimp, olives, etc. applied with frilled toothpicks.

5. Set dish filled with shrimp cocktail sauce into hollow of loaf. Set loaf upright on a dinner plate garnished with parsley.

CHEESE FONDUE

¼ lb. Swiss cheese,
  cubed or grated
¼ lb. Cheddar cheese,
  cubed or grated
2 pts. dry white wine

pinch nutmeg
salt, white pepper
  to taste
garlic (optional)
2 Tbsp. kirsch

1. Bring wine to boil, add cheese and stir.

2. When smooth, add seasoning and kirsch. Do not burn.

Note:
Check the fondue information following Swiss Fondue for helpful hints.

SWISS FONDUE

¼ lb. Emmentaler cheese, diced

¾ lb. Gruyere cheese, diced

3 Tbsp. flour

1 clove garlic

2 cups dry white wine

1 Tbsp. lemon juice

3 Tbsp. kirsch

nutmeg, pepper

Italian or French bread (1 in. squares)

cornstarch (if necessary)

Heat should vary in preparing Fondue. Low heat 120°, moderate heat 180°, and hot 212°.

1. Rub fondue pan with garlic.

2. Add wine.

3. Warm wine (do not boil).

4. Dredge the cheese in flour.

5. Add cheese gradually to wine, stirring constantly.

6. Increase the heat.

7. Flavor with pepper and nutmeg.

8. Add kirsch and lemon juice.

9. Keep the fondue bubbling, with low heat.

10. Keep heat very low.

11. Dip bread cubes (crust also, if desired) in fondue with long forks.

12. If thickening is needed, add cornstarch and wine. Wine should be warm when added.

13. No cold drinks should be served with fondue.

14. Finish with tea or warm apple cider.

Serves 4.

Serving Suggestion:
Fondue is excellent when served with smoked ham or sausage, followed by apple.

The idea of fondue dates back to the days when the European family meal was cooked in one pot which went from the hearth to the table. Everyone helped themselves with spoon, knife, bread or whatever utensil was available. Individual dishes were only for the very rich until the 17th century when plates and forks became fashionable. The ingenious Swiss devised cheese fondue to make use of scraps of old cheese that had dried out and to soften bread that had become too hard to eat.

The secret of cheese fondue is in the selection and heating of the cheeses. Use only natural cheese—not processed. Swiss is preferred to American as the imported cheeses are more mature than the domestic. Cook the cheese over very low heat or it may become stringy. Then keep the cheese hot, but not too hot or it will become tough.

Urge guests to swirl the cheese when they dunk their bread cubes—it keeps the fondue well mixed. And when it's nearly gone, a brown crust will form on the bottom of the dish. Some fondue lovers think this is the best part. Don't throw it away—enjoy it!

BATTER SHRIMP

1½ lbs. of frozen
   shrimp, cooked
2 cups of flour
2 eggs

½ cup milk
oil for deep frying
salt and pepper

1. Blend eggs and milk together, add flour and seasoning.

2. Roll shrimp in flour, then in batter and deep fry until
golden brown at 375°.

Serves 4.

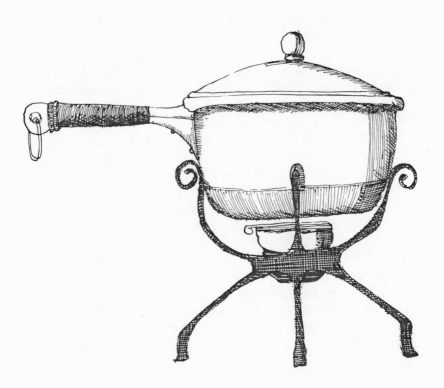

Chapter 11

Liquid Refreshments to Sip or Chew

Party menus deserve special soups and beverages like Irish coffee and vichyssoise. But don't save them just for company. Use these party recipes to brighten everyday meals, too. Even breakfast is sunnier with surprising strawberry-orange juice.

IRISH COFFEE

CREAM—rich as an Irish brogue (whipping cream)
COFFEE—strong as a friendly hand
SUGAR—sweet as the tongue of a rogue (brown sugar)
WHISKEY—smooth as the wit of the land

1. Heat a stemmed whiskey goblet with boiling water.

2. Pour in 1 jigger of Irish whiskey, the only whiskey with the smooth taste and full body needed.

3. Add 1 tsp. of brown sugar.

4. Fill goblet with hot, strong, black coffee to within 1 in. of the brim.

5. Stir to dissolve sugar.

6. Top off to brim with cream whipped to a soft peak, so

that the cream floats on top. Do not stir after adding cream, as the true flavor is obtained by drinking the hot coffee and whiskey through the cream.

Coffee, the most popular American drink today, was an invention of the Ethiopians during the 9th century. Legend has it that a goatherder saw his goats acting very frisky after eating the berries of an evergreen bush. He ate a few berries himself and liked the feeling. How the berries got from the bush to the coffee pot is anyone's guess. They weren't ground until 1400 and the world's first coffee house opened in Constantinople in 1475.

Coffee has had a most precarious history. It was first forbidden by orthodox Moslem priests as being intoxicating and in the 16th century the Roman Catholic Church censured it. But its popularity outweighed the objections of authority and its usage spread throughout the world. By 1725, London had two thousand coffee houses. The clientele was strictly male so they were not at all popular with the women who sat at home while their husbands gathered with the boys to drink coffee. It took the German women to invent the Kaffeeklatsch, a social event for both sexes. Coffee remained popular in England until the 19th century when its cost became too high and the English turned to tea for cheaper stimulation.

Today, Americans drink more than twenty-five billion gallons of coffee each year—nearly three cups a day for the average person.

TOM & JERRYS

6 eggs, room temperature   1 lb. sugar, superfine
1 tsp. allspice   pinch cream of tartar
1 tsp. nutmeg   **brandy and rum (6 oz. each)**

1. Separate egg whites from yolks. Add pinch cream of tartar to whites and whip until peaks form (about 8 times volume) then gradually add ½ lb. sugar.

2. Add pinch cream of tartar to yolks and whip same as whites, but only until triple in volume when done. Gradually add remaining sugar. Add allspice and nutmeg and mix well into egg yolks.

3. Place egg yolks in large serving bowl then carefully fold in egg whites until mixed and serve as follows:

   Pour ½ oz. rum and ½ oz. brandy in cup. Add Tom & Jerry batter until cup is ¾ filled, then finish cup by adding hot water. Sprinkle with nutmeg.

Serves 12.

Recipes for Tom and Jerry batter, like any food, can have a dozen variations. We've included two here to give you a choice of methods and flavors.

TOM & JERRY BATTER

1 qt. marshmallow topping   1 tsp. nutmeg
4 eggs, separated   1 tsp. cinnamon
½ tsp. cloves

1. Beat egg yolks until stiff.

2. Add marshmallow slowly and continue beating.

3. Add other ingredients and beat until smooth.

4. To serve, place in a mug:
   3 Tbsp. batter
   1 oz. brandy
   1 oz. rum

Add boiling water and stir.

007 COCKTAIL

8 oz. brandy   1 qt. chipped ice
4 oz. triple sec   1 can mandarin oranges
1 bottle champagne

1. Combine brandy, triple sec, and chipped ice in large glass or silver bowl.

2. Add 1 small can of mandarin oranges.

3. Add 1 bottle of champagne a few minutes before serving. Serve in 4 oz. punch cups.

Serves 10 to 12.

STRAWBERRY ORANGE JUICE

3 cups of fresh or frozen orange juice
3 cups of fresh or frozen strawberries

Combine 3 cups of strawberries and 3 cups of orange juice, both well chilled. Force the mixture through a sieve or puree in a blender. Sweeten to taste, if necessary.

Chef's Tip:
The simplest method is to use both frozen orange juice and frozen strawberries. Use 1 can of frozen orange juice and combine with 1 can of water in blender. Set aside. Then combine 1 package of frozen strawberries with 1 can of water (using the same can which contained the orange juice) in the blender. Mix the strawberry juice with the orange juice. Serve chilled.

Serves 6 happy people.

Note:
If desired, add 1 oz. vodka to each serving. Makes things even happier!

VELVET PUNCH

1 qt. sherbert (any flavor)   3 qts. ginger ale
4 dashes of angostura   1 qt. shaved ice
   bitters

1. Combine sherbert and ginger ale stirring until creamy.

2. Add ice a few minutes before serving.

Serves 20.

VICHYSSOISE

12 med. potatoes
3 leeks
1 med. onion
2 bay leaves

1 cup cream (half & half)
3 Tbsp. chopped chives
1 sprig parsley

1. Peel potatoes, chop leeks and onion. Place with bay leaves in saucepan, cover with water and boil until reduced to pulp consistency.

2. Remove bay leaves. Push potato mixture through a strainer. Add fresh cream and chopped chives. Serve either hot or cold. Decorate with fresh parsley.

Serves 6.

Pronounce this great American classic "visheeswahz" and don't forget that last "z" sound. It was the invention of Louis Diat for the opening of the Ritz Carlton Hotel on Madison Avenue in New York City in 1910. He named it after his hometown near Vichy, the French spa.

Vichyssoise is one of a number of "foreign" foods that are really American innovations. Swiss steak, Russian dressing and chop suey are a few more that are as American as Mom and apple pie.

GAZPACHO
(A Cold Soup)

3 finely chopped garlic
  cloves
1 peeled green pepper
2 red pimentoes
3 fresh tomatoes, peeled
  (squeeze out seeds before
  putting in blender)

2 cups white breadcrumbs
1 cup olive oil
2 qt. water
pinch of salt
pinch of cayenne
toasted white bread
  croutons

1. Pour ½ cup of water into blender and then add the garlic, pepper, pimentoes and tomatoes. Mix well.

2. Add breadcrumbs, olive oil and mix, then add remaining water.

3. Season with salt and cayenne according to taste. Serve with croutons.

Serves 10.

FRUIT SOUP

¼ cup sugar
2 cups orange juice
1 cup water
1 Tbsp. cornstarch
¼ cup water
juice of 1 lemon
¼ cup canned pitted
  cherries, drained

¼ cup maraschino cherries
1 Tbsp. raisins
¼ cup canned peaches,
  drained and diced
¼ cup mandarin oranges,
  drained

1. Bring sugar, water and orange juice to boil. Combine water and cornstarch. Add to orange mixture to thicken. Cool.

2. Add lemon juice and fruit. Chill well.

3. Serve in glass cups.

Serves 6 to 8.

Chef's Tip:
Serve with a sprig of mint or scoop of sherbet in soup or on the side.

Chapter 12

Popovers That Do!

*A little showmanship can get you most anything —
including compliments. Try these absolutely fool-proof,
never-fail popovers anytime you want to show off just a
bit. Guests will think you're pure genius and your family
will gaze upon you with new admiration. Who knows,
from a little popover, mink might grow!*

POPOVERS

2 eggs   1 cup flour
1 cup milk   ½ tsp. salt

1. Break eggs into a pitcher or lipped bowl so batter will be easy to pour into greased custard cups. Add milk and flour that has been sifted with salt. Mix well. Disregard lumps.

2. Fill the popover cups ¾ full. **Put into cold oven** and then set control at 450°. Bake 40 minutes.

Makes 8 to 12.

Chef's Tip:
1. Put custard cups on a cookie sheet for easier handling.

2. Do not open oven door while baking or popovers will collapse.

3. Popovers can be reheated at a later date at 350°. Just reheat until hot and crisp.

4. Batter may be made hours ahead of time. Store covered in refrigerator. Before baking, mix batter with a spoon. Add 5 minutes to baking time to insure crispness.

5. If you use muffin tins, fill alternate wells for larger popovers.

Chapter 13

For Breakfast Lovers

Breakfast can be the loveliest meal of the day. Given proper care, it can be the glorious start of a special day or a leisurely mid-morning brunch with friends. Save these recipes for some lazy weekend when you have time to fuss with breakfast.

DANISH EGG CAKE

4 oz. thick sliced bacon
  (2 slices)
1 small tomato, cut into
  6 wedges
3 green onions, diced

2 raw eggs
2 tsp. half & half
1 tsp. flour
1 cooked potato, diced
salt and pepper to taste

Preheat oven to 325°.

1. Whip eggs, flour, half & half, salt and pepper, and green onions in a bowl.

2. Saute bacon in a small frying pan until almost done, reduce heat and add egg mixture. Let simmer until it starts to set, then garnish with the tomato and potato. Place in a 325° oven approximately 5 minutes.

Serve right from the skillet.

Serves 1.

EGGS BENEDICT ET CETERA

Sauce Hollandaise:
1 cup butter (2 sticks)
5 Tbsp. fresh lemon juice
dash of salt
4 egg yolks (beaten well)

2 English muffins
(4 halves), toasted
4 slices Canadian bacon
or ham, broiled

4 paper thin slices of
truffles (optional)
4 poached eggs

1. Melt butter in double boiler under slow heat **allowing no boiling.**

2. Beat egg yolks well over similar heat adding butter slowly to begin with, increasing volume progressively. Stir ingredients until thickened to desired consistency.

3. Keep sauce in double boiler in warm water (must not boil). Should it thicken, add hot water or more lemon if desired, to bring sauce back to desired emulsion.

4. Poach eggs: In a skillet have enough water to cover eggs. Add ¼ tsp. vinegar for each cup of water. Bring water to just below boiling point. Break 1 egg at a time in a cup or saucer and put carefully into water. When all eggs are in, return heat to simmering point, let stand to desired firmness. (Trim with cutter, if desired, to fit muffin.) Make sure to drain all water off eggs before setting on just broiled ham slices which have now been added to the toasted muffin. Cover eggs liberally with sauce and if desired add truffle for finishing touch.

This dish can be served individually (2 eggs per person for

lunch) or it may be put on a serving platter with appropriate garnish.

Serves 2 to 4.

Note:
Variations to Sauce Hollandaise which can be used with poached eggs.

1. Add 1 tsp. of curry powder for Curry Hollandaise.

2. Add 1 tsp. of anchovy paste to make Sauce Arlésienne.

NANCY'S QUICK HOLLANDAISE SAUCE

1 can cream of chicken   ¼ cup mayonnaise
  soup   1 Tbsp. lemon juice

1. Mix all ingredients together in a saucepan and heat.

Serve over broccoli, asparagus, use in Eggs Benedict, or any dish in which you use Hollandaise Sauce.

Serves 6.

Chef's Tip:
Sauce may be stored in refrigerator for up to a week. Reheat before serving.

EGGS FLORENTINE

2 eggs, poached
½ pkg. frozen leaf spinach
  (cooked according
  to directions and
  drained well)

1 cup Lenten-Bechamel
½ cup fresh cream
½ cup grated Gruyere
  and Parmesan cheese
2 Tbsp. melted butter

Preheat oven to 450°.

1. Make Mornay sauce by mixing Lenten-Bechamel and cream in saucepan. Boil down to ⅓ cup. Add cheeses and mix well. Add butter and strain.

2. Arrange poached eggs on drained spinach in individual baking dishes. Pour Mornay sauce over eggs and spinach.

3. Sprinkle with butter and more Parmesan cheese.

4. Brown quickly in very hot oven.

Serves 1 to 2.

Chef's Tip:
To make Lenten-Bechamel, mix 2 Tbsp. flour and 2 Tbsp. butter in a saucepan over moderate heat. Stir constantly until blended, then add 1½ cups boiling milk, pinch of nutmeg, salt and pepper to taste. Cook until thoroughly blended.

BIRCHEMUESSLI
(A Swiss Health Breakfast)

2 cups oatmeal
8 cups of milk
1 lb. of fresh fruit

1 pt. yogurt
1 pt. cream, whipped

1. Cook the oatmeal in milk. Cool slightly.

2. Add the chopped fresh fruit. Add the yogurt.

3. Fold in ¾ of the freshly whipped cream.

4. Spoon into serving dishes. Decorate with a few pieces of the chopped fruit, and the remaining whipped cream. Serve hot.

Serves 6.

Yogurt, according to some historians, is more than 3500 years old. American yogurt is much thicker than that of Europe and the Mideast, and is made only of cows' milk, while the foreign versions are often made of goats' or water buffalo milk.

QUICHE A LA JENNIFER

pastry dough for 1 crust
4 slices of cooked bacon, crumbled
1 small onion, sliced and sauteed in bacon fat
2 oz. paper thin Swiss cheese
2 oz. paper thin ham slices
4 raw eggs, beaten
1 cup (8 oz.) warm coffee cream
nutmeg and salt to taste
2 tsp. flour
2 oz. grated Cheddar cheese
2 oz. chopped spinach, canned or frozen
2 oz. sliced mushrooms, fresh or canned

Preheat oven to 425°.

1. Line a 9 in. pie tin with pastry dough and bake at 425° for approximately 10 minutes. Remove from oven and turn oven down to 350°.

2. Set a thin layer of ham on bottom of pie crust, then a layer of Swiss cheese, then a layer of bacon and spinach and onion, and then the rest of the ham and Swiss cheese.

3. Mix the beaten eggs with the cream and sprinkle in the flour while stirring. Season with nutmeg and salt, and pour over layers in the pie tin. Let stand for 10 minutes. Sprinkle with the Cheddar cheese and mushrooms, and bake in 350° oven for 20 minutes, or until firm.

For variations of this Quiche, try flaked crabmeat or diced shrimp, add a tsp. of chopped chives, reduce the amount of cream to 6 oz. and add 2 oz. of sweet vermouth or white wine.

Serves 6 to 8.

QUICHE LORRAINE

pie dough for 1 crust
⅔ cup diced ham
⅔ cup diced cheese
   (American or Swiss)
⅓ cup onion, finely
   chopped

butter
dash of nutmeg,
   salt and pepper
1 Tbsp. chopped parsley
3 eggs, beaten
⅔ cup milk

Preheat oven to 350°.

1. Roll pie dough to ¼ in. thickness. Line pie tin.

2. Sprinkle ham and cheese on top of crust in pie tin.

3. Saute chopped onion in butter. Spread over ham and cheese.

4. Combine nutmeg, parsley, salt and pepper with beaten eggs and milk. Pour over ham and cheese. Bake for 30 minutes.

Serves 6.

Chef's Tip:
Nice luncheon idea as well as breakfast or supper. If time element is a problem, prepare entire recipe in advance with exception of adding the milk and egg mixture. Refrigerate until ready to bake and then add the milk and eggs.

Breakfast has had a variable history of popularity. In the early Middle Ages, breakfast was bread and ale. Dinner was served at nine in the morning. A big breakfast with lots of meat and fish was an English tradition from the 19th century when eating lunch was unfashionable. World War II rationing helped change that.

Americans have more than sixty packaged breakfast foods to choose from thanks to the Kellogg brothers, C. W. Post and the Reverend Sylvester W. Graham, who all pioneered the light, modern breakfast we know too well. Kellogg's Corn Flakes, Post Grape-Nuts and Graham flour were the initial products. Dr. Harvey Kellogg created the thin flakes of corn for a patient of his with false teeth. Grape-Nuts were originally called "Elijah's Manna" and were developed by Post who was plagued with ulcers. Graham believed that bran should be left in flour to help maintain digestive regularity and paved the way for Graham crackers.

CHRISTMAS COFFEE CAKE
(German)

1 qt. scalded milk,
   slightly cooled
1 Tbsp. lard
1 heaping Tbsp. butter
2 cakes fresh yeast
½ cup warm water
2 eggs, well beaten

1 cup sugar
1 cup raisins, cut fine
½ cup citron, cut fine
1 heaping tsp. cardamon
1 tsp. salt
4 cups sifted flour
   (or more to make dough)

Preheat oven to 350°.

1. Dissolve yeast in water.

2. Add lard, butter and salt to hot milk.

3. Then add eggs, sugar, raisins, citron and cardamon. Let cool.

4. Add yeast and enough flour to mix stiff, like bread.

5. Set dough in warm place. Cover and let rise to double in bulk.

6. Mold into two loaves and let rise again.

7. Bake until done, at least 60 minutes.

Chapter 14

A Thin Chapter

It is difficult to talk about food and dieting in the same breath. But if you must diet (and don't we all, occasionally) then do it with a flair!

LOW CALORIE LUNCHEON
(475 calories)

Whole artichoke with lemon butter
(more lemon than butter)

Ris de Veau Braise (braised sweetbreads)

New peas and shallots

Sorbet au Benedictine (low calorie
sherbet with a touch of Benedictine)

BRAISED SWEETBREADS

1 lb. sweetbreads
1 tsp. salt
1 Tbsp. lemon juice
1 sprig thyme
1 small bay leaf
1 sprig marjoram
3 sprigs parsley

1 thin slice onion
½ cup Madeira cooking
   wine
1 cup brown sauce
few grains pepper
2 Tbsp. each butter
   and bacon fat

1. Clean sweetbreads under cold running water. Add to 1 quart water that has been boiled 5 minutes with salt, lemon juice, thyme, bay leaf, marjoram, parsley and onion. Cook sweetbreads gently 5 minutes. Drain.

2. Plunge sweetbreads into cold water or allow to stand about 10 minutes. Remove skin and membrane and break into 1 in. pieces.

3. Melt 2 Tbsp. butter and 2 Tbsp. bacon fat in fry pan. Toss sweetbreads in fry pan and lightly brown. Add ¼ cup Madeira wine.

4. Meanwhile, heat 1 cup homemade brown sauce or canned beef gravy with the remaining ¼ cup wine. Add a few grains of pepper. Pour sauce over sweetbreads and serve.

Serves 4.

Chapter 15

Just Desserts

The old show business axiom "leave them laughing" holds true for dinner guests, too. Whether it is cool, refreshing fruit or something more ornate, dessert should be pure pleasure. Choose one that compliments your menu. Then enjoy your own just dessert—a round of applause from happy diners.

LEMON CRISP COOKIES

1 pkg. commercial lemon cake mix
½ cup cooking oil
2 beaten eggs
¼ tsp. vanilla
1 tsp. grated lemon peel
60 pecan halves

Preheat oven to 350º.

1. Mix and stir all ingredients (except pecans) until creamy.

2. Drop by teaspoonful on ungreased cookie sheet. Place pecan half in center of each cookie and bake 10 to 12 minutes.

Yield:
4 to 5 dozen 2 to 2½ in. cookies.

FATTIGMAD BAKKELSE

yolks of 10 eggs
¾ cup of sugar
1 cup of heavy cream

flour
whites of 2 eggs
½ tsp. of cardamon

1. Beat egg whites and mix with other ingredients. Use as little flour as possible to roll out thin.

2. Cut in diamond shapes. Slit in middle—pull one corner through center slit and deep fry in lard until golden brown.

3. Drain and sprinkle with powdered sugar.

Yield 10 dozen.

Here's a bit of food trivia that should astound your dinner guests. That first Thanksgiving dinner we all celebrate with such relish, was really a breakfast. And for dessert, the Indian brave, Quadequina, served the colonists a bushel of popped popcorn—the first they had ever tasted.

BERLINERKRANSER

2 raw egg yolks
2 hard-boiled egg yolks
½ cup sugar

1 cup butter
2 cups flour

Preheat oven to 300°.

1. Work well together the raw and hard-boiled egg yolks.

2. Add the sugar and work in the butter, alternating with flour to form a smooth dough.

3. Roll with the hands, into a long roll. Cut into about 30 pieces. Form each of them into a little roll.

4. Make a circle of each roll, crossing the ends. Dip each into slightly beaten egg whites, then into coarse sugar. Bake to a delicate brown for 10 to 15 minutes.

ZABAGLIONE

6 eggs, separated
3 Tbsp. of your favorite
 clear liqueur (For
 example: white creme
 d'menthe, white creme de
 cacao, Grand Marnier,
 annisette, etc.)

6 non-calorie sweetener
 tablets, crushed

1. Beat egg yolks with a rotary beater in top of a double
   boiler. Beat in liqueurs and sweetener tablets.

2. Place over hot (not boiling) water and cook, beating
   constantly until mixture is thick and light.

3. Beat egg whites until stiff, but not dry and fold into the
   yolk mixture.

Serve warm in sherbet glasses.

Serves 6.

CHOCOLATE FONDUE

Melt ¼ lb. bittersweet chocolate in a small fondue pot.
According to taste, dip slices or wedges of fresh fruit and
small cubes of sponge cake into the chocolate with
fondue forks.

Slices of fresh pineapple, peaches, apples, bananas, and
pears are the most popular fruits used for dipping. Be
sure to completely cover the fruit with the chocolate
when dipping and then let cool for a few seconds before
tasting.

Chef's Tips:
Place cut fruit in a sieve and dunk quickly into orange
juice to prevent discoloration. Do not soak. Drain well.

Use Swiss melting chocolate for best results.

If desired, thin melted chocolate with ¼ cup cream.

Add 1 oz. kirsch or Cointreau for added flavor.

Milk chocolate was first introduced in Switzerland in
1876. The Swiss melting chocolate suggested for this
fondue is Toberlone, which is made with honey, crushed
almonds and flavoring.

CREPES SUZETTE

⅔ cup flour
1 Tbsp. sugar
pinch of salt
2 eggs

2 egg yolks
1¾ cups milk
2 Tbsp. melted butter
1 Tbsp. rum or cognac

1. Sift together flour, sugar and salt.

2. Beat together eggs and egg yolks. Add to dry ingredients.

3. Add milk and stir until smooth. Stir in melted butter and rum. Cover and refrigerate for 2 hours before using.

4. To cook the crepes, melt just enough butter in a hot pan to coat it thinly. Pour in a thin layer of crepe batter. The crepe should set and become brown in about 1 minute. Turn it over to brown the other side. Remove and set aside until serving time.

Serve with the following sauce:

SAUCE FOR CREPES SUZETTE

½ cup sugar
⅛ lb. sweet butter
8 oz. fresh orange juice
peel of orange (include some of the yellow)
peel of lemon (include some of the yellow)

1. Caramelize sugar lightly, making sure it does not burn. Add orange juice, peel and butter, Reduce to about a third of liquid.

2. Add crepes one by one, turning them over so they are well saturated with the sauce.

3. Pour over 1 oz. each of Benedictine, Yellow Chartreuse and Cognac. Ignite and serve quickly, pouring sauce over.

Makes 12-5 in. crepes.

CHERRIES JUBILEE

1-No. 2 can pitted large
   cherries
2 Tbsp. cornstarch

1 oz. cognac
2 pts. ice cream

1. Strain cherry juice and bring to a boil. Slightly thicken with cornstarch.

2. Heat cherries in another pan and pour cognac over them. Ignite the cherries and shake pan to distribute flame over entire pan.

3. Add thickened sauce to mixture. Bring to a boil and laddle jubilee over vanilla ice cream in dessert dishes and serve.

Serves 6.

Truly American originated desserts are apple pie, Lady Baltimore cake, pecan pie, shoo-fly pie, apple pandowdy, strawberry shortcake and pumpkin pie. The ice cream cone was invented at the St. Louis World's Fair in 1904 and the ice cream soda originated at Philadelphia's Franklin Institute in 1874.

STRAWBERRIES ROMANOFF

2 pt. boxes fresh
  strawberries
1 pt. fresh whipping
  cream

1½ oz. orange liqueur
2 Tbsp. sugar
red food coloring

1. Hull and wash strawberries. Reserve 6 large berries for decoration and soak remainder in 1 oz. of the liqueur and sugar for at least 30 minutes.

2. Whip cream to a heavy smooth consistency and then divide into 2 bowls. Stiff whip one bowl and set aside.

3. Add enough red food coloring to the cream in the second bowl to a make a pink color. Add ½ oz. of the liqueur and sweeten to taste.

4. Spoon the pink cream over strawberries in dessert dishes. Decorate with the stiffly whipped cream and top with a whole strawberry.

Serves 6.

Chef's Tip:
To distribute the sugar and liqueur over the strawberries shake each over berries in a bowl. Cover and gently turn bowl to mix berries without bruising.

SCHWARZWÄLDER TORTE

9 in. butter sponge cake
1 med. can of sour
   pitted cherries (set aside
   2 Tbsp. cherry juice)
¼ tsp. cornstarch

1 qt. whipping cream
2 Tbsp. cherry juice
3 Tbsp. white sugar
1 lb. sweet chocolate

1. Split sponge cake into 3 layers.

2. Cook cherries with cornstarch to a thick consistency. Let cool, and pour this on top of one layer of cake, which will be the top layer.

3. Whip 1 qt. of whipping cream with 3 Tbsp. of sugar, into stiff peaks, and pour in 2 Tbsp. of cherry juice, and mix well.

4. Arrange a quarter of this mixture on top of one layer of cake. Place another layer on top of this. Put half of the whipped cream mixture on this, and add the third layer on top. Spread with the rest of the whipping cream mixture.

5. Shave chocolate on top of cake. Refrigerate, or serve at once.

GRAHAM CRACKER LOAF

28 graham crackers,
  crushed
½ tsp. salt
½ cup shortening
3 eggs, slightly beaten

½ cup sugar
1½ tsp. baking powder
1 cup chopped nut meats
½ cup milk

Preheat oven to 375º.

1. Mix sugar, salt and baking powder with graham crackers that have been crushed very fine (should be about 2¼ cups of crumbs).

2. Cut in the shortening until mixture resembles texture of coarse cornmeal.

3. Cut in the nuts and add the eggs, slightly beaten, and milk. Blend this very well.

4. Pour into a greased loaf pan.

Bake until loaf is browned and springs back when gently touched. (About 50 to 60 minutes.)

Makes 1 loaf.

The Persians were the first big sweet-lovers and because of it early Persian rulers became obese. Only the very rich could afford sugar, so obesity became a status symbol. Honey was the most commonly used sweetener throughout history until sugar became reasonably priced and readily available in the late 1800's. Honey is not native to North America and was brought to New England from Europe in the mid-1600's. The Indians promptly named the foreign honeybee "white man's fly."

DANISH RICE AND ALMOND PUDDING

1 cup converted rice
2 cups milk
¾ cup sugar
1 tsp. salt
½ cup slivered almonds
1 Tbsp. vanilla extract

1 pt. whipping cream,
  whipped
1 oz. gelatin (dissolved
  in ½ cup hot water
  and cooled)

Preheat oven to 350°.

1. Rinse the rice in water.

2. Bring the milk, sugar, salt and vanilla to a boil. Add the rice. Stir approximately 1 minute. Place covered in 350° oven for 25 minutes.

3. While the rice is cooking, bring almonds to a boil in water. Remove from heat and drain off water.

4. When rice is cooked, let cool. Mix in gelatin and let stand 5 minutes. Add whipped cream and almonds. Chill. Serve with hot cherry sauce.

Serves 4.

CHERRY SAUCE

1 can pitted Bing cherries
¼ cup sugar

2 tsp. cornstarch
¼ cup orange juice

1. Bring the cherries with juice to a boil. Add the sugar.

2. Dissolve the cornstarch in the orange juice and add to the cherries. Simmer 2 minutes.

APPLE CAKE

6 to 8 oz. Holland rusk or
   Zweiback, crushed
4 Tbsp. granulated sugar
2 eggs, separated (beat
   the whites until frothy)
1 Tbsp. vanilla extract
9 in. layer cake pan,
   lined with pie dough

3 oz. butter, melted
3 oz. chopped almonds,
   fine
1 lemon, grated rind only
1 lb. apples, peeled and
   sliced

Preheat oven to 250°.

1. Line 9 in. layer cake pan with pie dough.

2. Boil the apples with half the sugar and the vanilla, in very little water, until done. Let cool and place on pie dough in the bottom of the cake pan.

3. Mix the Holland rusk with the remaining 2 Tbsp. sugar, almonds, egg yolks, melted butter, and lemon rind. Mix very thoroughly, then add the beaten egg whites. Spread this mixture over the apples and bake for about 30 minutes.

Serve with whipped cream or ice cream.

Serves 6 to 8.

LEMON PUDDING

3 egg yolks
3 egg whites
3 oz. sugar
rind of 2 lemons

juice of 2 lemons
1 oz. gelatin, dissolved
in small amount of water

1. Beat the egg yolks until white, adding sugar slowly. Add lemon juice and rind. Next, add the gelatin and let stand.

2. Beat the egg whites to a stiff froth, add to the egg yolks a little at a time.

3. Chill, stirring once in a while until pudding starts to set.

4. Pour into a large glass bowl and chill for 1 hour. Decorate with orange slices and whipped cream.

Serves 4.

RUM APPLE CAKE WITH WHIPPED CREAM

6 apples   2 Tbsp. melted butter
1 cup water   3 Tbsp. sugar
½ tsp. cinnamon   2 Tbsp. rum
½ cup sugar   1 pt. whipping cream
13 Zwieback crackers

1. Peel, core and quarter apples. Boil slowly in water with cinnamon and ½ cup sugar until soft but firm.

2. Crush 10 Zwieback crackers and mix with butter, 1 Tbsp. sugar. Place in bottom of 9 in. spring form pan.

3. Arrange apples close together on top of cracker mixture and sprinkle with 1 Tbsp. rum.

4. Whip cream with 2 Tbsp. sugar and 1 Tbsp. rum. Smooth over apples.

5. Crush 3 more crackers and sprinkle over whipped cream.

6. Chill cake for 2 hours.

Serves 8 to 10.

STRAWBERRY WHIPPED CREAM CAKE

Egg Mixture
2½ cups sugar
1 tsp. salt
3 cups egg yolks, room temperature
¼ cup egg whites

1. Heat eggs to 85° or hand warm to body temperature. Whip at a medium speed for about 25 minutes, adding sugar and salt slowly. (If you peak batter, and it falls slowly, it is ready.)

Flour Mixture
2 cups cake flour
1 tsp. baking powder

1. Sift these together two times.

Milk Mixture
1 cup milk
½ cup butter
½ tsp. vanilla

1. Heat milk. Melt butter in milk, and then add vanilla.

Preheat oven to 370°.

1. Fold alternately, flour mixture and milk mixture into the egg mixture. Do not whip this entire mixture, just blend well.

2. Pour batter (at least 8 oz. in each) into three 8 in. round pans and bake until golden brown. (About 15 to 20 minutes.) Cake should spring back when lightly touched with finger.

Layer and top with strawberry mix.

STRAWBERRY MIX

1 qt. whipping cream   2 cups chopped and
1 oz. cherry brandy   sugared strawberries

1. Whip cream well. Add 1 oz. of cherry brandy.

2. Put sugared strawberries into half of the whipped cream and stack 3 cake layers, spreading strawberry whipped cream mixture between them.

3. Use the rest of the plain whipped cream to decorate and cover rest of cake. Use your imagination and creative fantasy to create a pleasing effect. Fresh whole strawberries may be used on top also, for an added festive touch.

This cake should be refrigerated.

MOTHER'S CHOCOLATE CAKE

4 squares of unsweetened
  dark chocolate
½ cup lard
1 cup boiling water
2 cups all-purpose flour
1½ tsp. baking soda
½ tsp. salt
2 cups sugar
2 beaten eggs
1 tsp. vanilla
½ cup sour milk

Preheat oven to 400°.

1 Melt chocolate and lard in boiling water. Mix well and let cool.

2. Meanwhile, sift flour, soda, salt and sugar together 3 times.

3. Add to chocolate mixture and mix well. Then add sour milk, eggs, vanilla and beat for 5 minutes.

4. Pour into large rectangular metal cake pan and bake in 400° oven for 25 minutes.

Frost with Mother's Caramel Icing.

MOTHER'S CARAMEL ICING

1⅓ cups light brown
  sugar
⅔ cup white sugar
⅔ cup cream
1 Tbsp. butter
8 large marshmallows
1 tsp. vanilla

1. Stir together sugars, cream and butter and boil until mixture reaches "soft ball" state (test by dropping ½ tsp. mixture in 1 cup cold water).

2. Remove from heat, add marshmallows and vanilla. Then beat (with rotary or electric beater) until creamy.

Yield:
Icing for Mother's Chocolate Cake, or for one 2-layered cake.

Cookbooks are the most popular reading material next to the Bible, yet published cookbooks with precise measurements are a recent innovation. The first recorded cookbook was compiled in the first century A. D. by a Roman named Apicius. He called it *Of Culinary Matters.*

By 1650, ladies kept handwritten "receipt" books to pass on to to their oldest daughters. Directions and measurements were usually vague and impossible for a beginner to follow. Then in 1896, Miss Fannie Merritt Farmer published *The Boston Cooking-School Cook Book* complete with standardized measurements and detailed instructions. Miss Farmer published that first edition at her own expense. It has been updated and reprinted many times since then and has sold millions of copies.

As some historians have said, the history of food is the history of the world. Nothing is more important to the survival and quality of life than the abundance and wise use of food.

Bon appetite! May all the cooking pots of your life be filled to overflowing with nourishments of the gods to please and fulfill you.

Acknowledgements

Our deepest thanks to the many outstanding chefs who have enhanced our enjoyment of eating and especially to...

John Sydney Logan
George Theros and the Kings Inn
Larry Tabone
Eberhard Werthmann
Tom Langlais
Sra. Coronado and La Casa Coronado
Reiko Weston and the Fuji-Ya
Clifford Warling and the Blue Horse
Louise Saunders and Charlies' Cafe Exceptionale
Hans Skalle and the Camelot
Chuck Combs
Fred Kalantari
Tommy Nakama

And special thanks to...

Harold Feder, Samuel S. Fisher and the Fisher Nut Company for making both words and nuts more enjoyable.

Lorraine F. Steiner for her fondness of food, her willingness to work and especially for her magnificent typing.

Robert F. Leren for lending his peerless adroitness for chirography and for some pretty clever words.

Roger W. Kline for art direction, page make-up suggestions and layout.

Lewis S. and Phyllis M. Igo for creating a lifelong interest in cookery.

KSTP-TV for providing the opportunity of presenting the talent of these experts in cookery to television audiences.

And to Roy Harris for counsel, encouragement, inspiration, et cetera.

Bibliography

Balsdon, J. P. V. D. *Roman Women: Their History and Habits.* (New York, The John Day Company, 1963.)

Beck, Simone, Bertholle, Louisette and Child, Julia. *Mastering the Art of French Cooking.* (New York, Alfred A. Knopf, 1963.)

Claiborne, Craig. *The New York Times Cook Book.* (New York and Evanston, Harper & Row, 1961.)

Fisher, M. F. K. *With Bold Knife and Fork.* (New York, G. P. Putnam's Sons, 1969.)

Hazelton, Nika Standen, and the Editors of TIME-LIFE BOOKS. *Foods of the World: The Cooking of Germany.* (New York, Time-Life Books, 1969.)

Hazelton, Nika Standen. *The Swiss Cookbook.* (New York, Atheneum, 1967.)

Montagne, Prosper. *Larousse Gastronomique.* (New York, Crown Publishers, Inc., 1961.)

Papashvily, Helen and George, and the Editors of TIME-LIFE BOOKS. *Foods of the World: Russian Cooking.* (New York, Time-Life Books, 1969.)

Perkins, Wilma Lord. *The All New Fannie Farmer Boston Cooking School Cookbook.* (Boston-Toronto, Little, Brown and Company, 1959.)

Trager, James. *The Foodbook.* (New York, Grossman Publishers, 1970.)

Index

Phyllis Jedlicka is a professional writer whose background includes radio, television, children's theater, magazines and advertising. She is also wild about good cooking (and good eating, too). A native Minneapolitan, Phyllis operates her own advertising/communications agency, Communications Et Cetera, Inc.

G. R. Cheesebrough operates a free-lance art studio in the Twin Cities. His work has appeared in local and national magazines, newspapers and books. He has had shows in New York, San Francisco, Los Angeles and throughout the midwest. Cheesebrough originals as well as limited edition prints hang in galleries throughout the United States. His work recently took on international scope in the form of tourist posters for Great Britain.